THE MODERN PSYCHOLOGICAL NOVEL

The Modern Psychological Novel

By LEON EDEL

The Universal Library
GROSSET & DUNLAP
NEW YORK

For
ROBERTA

INTRODUCTION
TO THE
UNIVERSAL LIBRARY EDITION

THIS BOOK was published a decade ago under the title of *The Psychological Novel* 1900–1950. Later, when it was reprinted in softcover, I renamed it *The Modern Psychological Novel*. I think that today, if it were possible to rename this book without creating the impression that I had written a new one, I would call it *Modes of Subjectivity in the Modern Novel*. But I hesitate to change the name a second time. In the interest of clarity I have resorted to a subtitle.

My original choice of "psychological" stemmed from my wish to use the widest category within which the stream-of-consciousness and internal monologue novel (by which I mean fiction *wholly* subjective) falls. I found the metaphor—the suggestion of consciousness as something flowing, like a stream—descriptive but imprecise, and I still feel that it does not really convey what happens in a novel when we are placed behind, instead of in front of, the eyes of a character. I am writing, moreover, not only about the literary representation of thought in its flowing and evanescent state, but about the representation within consciousness of sensory experience: as in the opening of *A Portrait of the Artist as a Young Man* or in Faulkner's picture of the arrested consciousness of the idiot Benjy in *The Sound and the Fury*. And then I was concerned also with the representation in literature of the process of association (as in Proust), and with Virginia Woolf's attempts to capture the color and content of a single moment, the whole spectrum of awareness of which we are capable. As there had been a movement dedicated to recording the realism of the outer world in the 19th century, so it was necessary to recognize the 20th century's search for inner reality. All this seemed to me a lively experimental adventure on the part of the narrative artists of our time, to which insufficient attention had been paid, save in certain isolated studies.

During earlier editions of this book I made two interesting discoveries. Neither is very important, but they deserve a passing mention. The first was that my attempt to explain and define the subjective novel was taken by certain novelists, among them C. P. Snow, as advocacy of the "stream of consciousness" in opposition to other kinds of novels; even as a curious concept exists among critics that my being the biographer of Henry James means that I want all novels to be "Jamesian." The absurdity of such assumptions need not be explained by one who has been attracted from the first to the experimental novel; and who has no sense of the English novel save as a remarkably elastic, self-renewing literary form, even when it regresses to older forms—even when it returns to its earliest epistolary form, or becomes as extravagantly "point of view" as in the *Alexandria Quartet.*

My second discovery was that bibliographers are apparently guided by titles rather than by the contents of a work. This volume has been faithfully listed in bibliographies dealing with literature and psychology. It has been ignored in bibliographies dealing with the stream-of-consciousness and the subjective novel. There are, so far as I know, only two other books dealing explicitly with this subject and these are concerned with definitions and historical and textual analysis of the stream-of-consciousness phenomenon in fiction—Robert Humphrey's *Stream of Consciousness in the Novel* (1954) and Melvin Friedman's *Stream of Consciousness: A Study of Literary Method* (1955): neither is concerned in any detail with the psychological aspect, or with the handling of the perceptual data, or with subjective modes other than the recording of flowing thought; although inevitably we deal with the same novelists. More recently there has also been a specialized treatise on *Bergson and the Stream of Consciousness Novel* by Shiv K. Kumar (1963). The present book differs from the others in its step-by-step account of what happens in fiction when the reader is asked to read it not in terms of external reality but from the inside-out. I have been astonished that certain novelists discussing the art of fiction in recent years lump *Ulysses* or *The Sound and the Fury* with the novel as written by Dickens, or Thackeray, E. M. Forster or D. H. Lawrence, or speak of Virginia Woolf as if she were merely another novelist in the long line since Samuel Richardson. There has been a singular failure to recognize that the Joycean novel belongs to a separate category of fiction within the art of the novel.

What I have tried to show—and largely from the reader's point of view—is that the modern subjective novelists cannot be read like their predecessors: that a whole new educational process in fictional reading is implied, from the moment the novel asks us to become a camera, as it were, and a recording apparatus as well.

I am happy on the occasion of this new edition to rectify the bibliographical status of my book, and I am taking advantage of the circumstance to add certain of my more recent studies in the field and my observations on the continuing experiments in fictional subjectivity at the midcentury. These form the entire section titled "Part Two: Modes of Subjectivity." The use of the stream-of-consciousness novel as a battle-cry by C. P. Snow, the subjective experiments of Lawrence Durrell, the advent of the *nouveau roman* in France, the reprinting of Conrad Aiken's brilliant experiments of a quarter of a century ago, and the use of the subjective mode on the stage by Arthur Miller in *After the Fall*—an instance of the direct fertilization of the drama by fiction—indicate quite clearly that the movement is far from "dead," as is sometimes claimed. To be sure we no longer have writers like Faulkner or Joyce or Mrs. Woolf. But other novelists have assimilated their techniques and integrated the old experiments into new ones.

In a sense this essay might be said to take up the novel where both Percy Lubbock, in *The Craft of Fiction*, and E. M. Forster, in *Aspects of the Novel*, left it. Mr. Lubbock, writing before *Ulysses*, took us as far as Henry James's "point of view." Mr. Forster, writing after Joyce's Odyssey in Dublin, was still too close to the period when *Ulysses* was either "fantasy" or "a dogged attempt to cover the universe with mud" to understand the full proportions of Joyce's achievement. It was left to Edmund Wilson (in *Axel's Castle*) to show us the symbolist roots of the contemporary novel and to give full weight to Joycean and Proustian attempts to recreate time past and time present. My debt to him will be readily recognized by readers of this book. I am deeply indebted also to Harry Levin's admirable study of James Joyce.

My grateful acknowledgments are due to Harold G. Files, Professor of English at McGill University in Montreal, who guided my early enthusiasm for the psychological novel; to R. P. Blackmur and E. B. O. Borgerhoff of Princeton University, who invited me to explore my subject at the Christian Gauss Seminar in Criticism, and to Joseph Prescott of Wayne University, whose studies in Joyce have led him to consider the wider problem of the "stream of consciousness" in fiction, and who also has been among the very few champions of the work of Dorothy Richardson. Finally I wish to express my appreciation to Howard Fertig, of Grosset and Dunlap, editor of the Universal Library, for valuable suggestions in the linking of the old and new material in this book.

Leon Edel

New York University
June 1964

CONTENTS

PART I

THE MODERN PSYCHOLOGICAL NOVEL

CHAPTER I

ATMOSPHERE OF THE MIND

ON THE eve of the First World War three novelists, unknown to each other, were writing works destined to have
a remarkable influence on the fiction of our century. In
France Marcel Proust, a sickly man and a semi-recluse,
deeply introspective and self-absorbed, published in 1913
the first two volumes of the eight-part work we know today as *Remembrance of Things Past*. While these volumes
were on the press, an Englishwoman, Dorothy Miller
Richardson, vigorously feminist and possessing a considerable awareness of the inner life of her mind, had begun to
write what would in the end be a twelve-part novel entitled *Pilgrimage*. The first volume—Miss Richardson
called each of the twelve a "chapter"—appeared in 1915,
the last in 1938. Between the launching of these two
ambitious works on both sides of the Channel, James
Joyce, an Irishman, then a teacher of English in the
Berlitz school at Trieste, began publishing in serial form
(in 1914) a novel entitled *A Portrait of the Artist as a Young
Man*. It was not part of a longer work, like Proust's or
Dorothy Richardson's. Yet it was destined to have an
important sequel that would mark a turning-point in the
imaginative literature of our time.

Thus, between 1913 and 1915, was born the modern
psychological novel—what we have come to call, in English letters, the stream-of-consciousness novel or the novel
of the silent, the internal monologue, and in French letters, the modern analytic novel, which, if not written as
flowing thought, sought the very atmosphere of the mind.

This was a coincidence indeed—that three writers, unknown to each other, three distinctly different talents and
temperaments, should, at the same time, have turned
fiction away from external to internal reality, from the

outer world that Balzac had charted a century before to
the hidden world of fantasy and reverie into which there
play constantly the life and perception of our senses.
There were striking similarities in these works, behind
their differences. They seemed to be essentially autobiographical. They contained an unusual infusion of the
language of poetry. Their very titles suggested, if we include *Ulysses* (which Joyce wrote after the *Portrait*), a
curious kinship of search, voyage, pilgrimage. Indeed,
all were voyages through consciousness. For the three
writers were aware, in extraordinary degree, of their feelings and sensations. They were capable, moreover, of
candid self-examination, to an extent uncommon even
among writers. All three seemed to write from an acute
need to cope with inner problems and project their inner
life before the world. This may be true of all artists; but
this time the traditional process of projecting the inner
experience into an imaginative narrative dealing with the
external world was not carried out. These novelists
sought to retain and record the "inwardness" of experience.

In the case of Proust, continual illness had fostered the
living and reliving of his novel within the tight walls of a
cork-lined room from which he tried to shut out the sound
and dust of the world—almost as if the room itself had
become his very mind in which thoughts could flow, un-
molested by the ruder temperatures and sharper lights of
the world outside. As in psycho-analysis the patient is
isolated from external stimuli that his mind may play
over his past and link it to the present, so Proust in his
sound-proofed isolation could practise his extraordinary
self-analysis. The present assailed him too violently; immediate experience erupted into allergies and the ills of
the flesh. In the past there was tranquillity—and discovery. By the process of remembering, he found himself.

Experience for Joyce took quite another form. Near-
blind from his childhood, he lived in a world of sound, in
the ceaseless clamour of the city of his youth, Dublin,
which he carried with him whether he was in Trieste, in
Zürich, or in Paris—and in the end all the cities blended

in an ever-increasing din, and their languages mingled, so that Joyce's mind became a Tower of Babel. Unlike Proust, however, Joyce wanted to catch the present, the immediate moment of perception—he called it an "epiphany," applying the religious word to his artist's vision. For Proust, time past could become time present, to fade immediately into the past again; for Joyce time present was all-important—a continuum of present, in which the past inevitably lingered.

Miss Richardson seems to have enjoyed better health than her male confrères, although we gather that she, too, had a sensitivity heightened by myopia. Her work speaks from a quieter and less dramatic life than that of Proust or Joyce, and it is accordingly more limited. Yet certain quiet intensities of her inner being clamoured to be set down, and her novel became an experiment to which she gave all her resources and her devotion. If she was the least artist of the three, she was an articulate vessel of feeling, and bent upon challenging the "masculine" novel. She set out to record the "point of view" of a woman, and she learned her craft in the process.

Proust began his novel as a direct narrative of memory:

For a long time I used to go to bed early. Sometimes, when I had put out my candle, my eyes would close so quickly that I had not even time to say "I'm going to sleep." And half an hour later the thought that it was time to go to sleep would awaken me; I would try to put away the book which, I imagined, was still in my hands, and to blow out the light; I had been thinking all the time, while I was asleep, of what I had just been reading, but my thoughts had run into a channel of their own, until I myself seemed actually to have become the subject of my book: a church, a quartet, the rivalry between François I and Charles V.

Dorothy Richardson's novel began quite conventionally:

Miriam left the gaslit hall and went slowly upstairs. The March twilight lay upon the landings, but the staircase was almost dark. The top landing was quite dark and silent. There was no one about. It would be quiet in her room. She could sit by the fire and be quiet and think things over until Eve and

13

Harriet came back with the parcels. She would have time to think about the journey and decide what she was going to say to the Fräulein.

Neither of these quiet openings gave any inkling that a major change in the art of fiction was under way. The reader would have to cover several pages before becoming aware that he was on the threshold of innovation: and even then there was some question whether there had been any serious departure from the least rigid of our literary forms—one that embraces works as different as *Tristram Shandy* and *The Ambassadors*. But there was no question of the novelty of James Joyce's opening of *A Portrait of the Artist as a Young Man*:

Once upon a time and a very good time it was there was a moocow coming down along the road and this moocow that was coming down along the road met a nicens little boy named baby tuckoo . . .

His father told him that story: his father looked at him through a glass: he had a hairy face.

He was baby tuckoo. The moocow came down the road where Betty Byrne lived: she sold lemon platt.

> O, the wild rose blossoms
> On the little green place.

He sang that song. That was his song.

> O, the green wothe botheth.

When you wet the bed, first it is warm then it gets cold. His mother put on the oilsheet. That had the queer smell.

His mother had a nicer smell than his father.

What the reader discovered, as he read on, was that these were not narratives in the traditional sense. The author (save in the case of Proust) seemed bent on effacing himself and confronting the reader with the direct mental experience of the characters. There were only occasional shifts from past to present, from present to past; what was happening seemed to occur largely at whatever moment the reader happened to be reading the story. This was a distinct departure from the way in which the conventional novels unrolled themselves in majestic leisure with the author constantly telling the

14

story and omniscient to the extent of knowing everything about his characters. This removal of the author from the scene—he remained often an intruder, but was no longer omnipresent—made necessary a significant shift in narrative: it created the need to use the memory of the characters to place the reader in a relationship with their past. There was no "story," no "plot." And above all, this kind of novel seemed to turn the reader into an author: it was he, ultimately, who put the story together, and he had to keep his wits about him to accumulate his data. The Christmas dinner at the Dedalus household, had it been told by Balzac, would have contained a catalogue of the household furnishings, the menu, and minute descriptions of those at the table. For this Joyce substituted the observations of the boy and the intensities of feeling of the elders: we come to know the Dedalus household not through its physical appearance but through the qualities of feeling that exist within it and their effect on the observant and sensitive Stephen. In *Pointed Roofs*, Miss Richardson gives us our data piecemeal: forty pages must be read before we discover that Miriam's last name is Henderson, and we learn that she is seventeen after half a hundred pages. The reader is enveloped in sensations and daydreams, even as in Proust he remains nearly always with the reminiscential narrator, thinking of all the beds he has slept in and wandering off into the world of Combray, to meet Monsieur Swann, or feel the anguish of the boy awaiting his mother's goodnight kiss, and finally to be led to the unrolling of the deliberate, introspective, searching narrative, spun like a spider's web from the moment that the madeleine is dipped into the tea. In Joyce, intermittently, one is inside the mind of the developing little boy with his bad eyesight, his acute sense of sound and smell:

There was the smell of evening in the air, the smell of the fields in the country where they digged up turnips to peel them and eat them when they went out for a walk to Major Barton's, the smell there was in the little wood beyond the pavilion where the gallnuts were.

The fellows were practising long shies and bowling lobs and

slow twisters. In the soft grey silence he could hear the bump of the balls: and from here and from there through the quiet air the sound of the cricket bats: pick, pack, pock, puck: like drops of water in a fountain falling softly in the brimming bowl.

We are nearly always with Stephen: and the *Portrait* of him is a portrait of his sensations and passions, as well as of his thoughts and his intellectual development.

2

This was a new kind of realism, unrelated to the fiction of Arnold Bennett or H. G. Wells or John Galsworthy, who had their vogue at the time that these major experiments in psychological fiction were being launched. It was an attempt in a more minute and thorough fashion than ever before to document the whole world of the senses and to catch fugitive thoughts in their progress through the mind—catch them, as Joyce was to do in *Ulysses*—in their very moment of flow. In other words, for the first time, these novelists were seeking to find words that would convey elusive and evanescent thought: not only the words that come to the mind, but the images of the inner world of fantasy, fusing with sounds and smells, the world of perceptual experience. And yet the attempts did not seem new to many critics who pointed out that writers of other centuries, in many countries, had set down the thoughts and reveries of their characters.

What difference, it might be asked, was there between what Joyce attempted and this description of thought in Dostoevsky?

"It must be the top drawer," he [Raskolnikov] reflected.
"So she carries the keys in a pocket on the right. All in one bunch on a steel ring. . . . And there's one key there, three times as big as all the others, with deep notches; that can't be the key of the chest of drawers . . . then there must be some other chest or strong-box . . . that's worth knowing. Strong-boxes always have keys like that . . . but how degrading it all is."

Yet there is a significant difference. It lies in the fact that this is merely unspoken speech and that it is Dostoevsky who tells us "he reflected." In other words, we have here not a flowing stream of thought but a narrator's report—the author being the narrator—of what is occurring in the mind of his character.

What, then, of the soliloquies of Shakespeare? Othello's great debate with himself at the moment when he must act, or Hamlet's

> To die, to sleep;
> To sleep; perchance to dream; ay, there's the rub;
> For in that sleep of death what dreams may come.

But these are organized monologues in which the mind presents reasoned and ordered thought, the "end-product" of the stream of consciousness, not the disordered stream itself. A better case might be made for the mad speeches of Lear, yet even these have that "reason in madness" of which Edgar speaks. Still better would be the following, in which Shakespeare attempts to render a chain of associations, flowing from a person into whose mind we are allowed briefly to penetrate. Quoted without the interruptions of other speakers, who on the stage offer a running commentary as the thoughts are revealed, this is what we get:

> Yet here's a spot. Out, damned spot! out, I say! One: two: why, then 'tis time to do't. Hell is murky. Fie, my lord, fie! a soldier and afeard? What need we fear who knows it, when none can call our power to account? Yet who would have thought the old man to have had so much blood in him? The thane of Fife had a wife: where is she now? What, will these hands ne'er be clean? No more o'that, my lord, no more o'that: you mar all with this starting. Here's the smell of blood still: all the perfumes of Arabia will not sweeten this little hand. Oh! oh! oh! Wash your hands; put on your night-gown; look not so pale: I tell you yet again, Banquo's buried; he cannot come out on's grave. To bed, to bed: there's knocking at the gate: come, come, come, come, give me your hand: what's done cannot be undone, to bed, to bed, to bed.

This is not "stream of consciousness" as we have come to know it in Joyce and Faulkner. It is, nevertheless, closer to it than other examples that have been cited out of the literature of the past. The element of discontinuity is here: there is a seeming mixture of the irrelevant and the relevant—and yet not a word is placed that is not *dramatically* relevant. In this instance, for so Shakespeare had to write it, Lady Macbeth's thoughts coincide with the memories of the audience: they have seen and heard everything that her tortured mind evokes in its somnolent articulateness: they can experience her guilt, her resolution, her courage, her doubt. The impression of a flow of thought is created. And the thoughts flow directly to us from the mind of the personage.

One can find many isolated examples in which writers of the past give us glimpses into the mind, furtive thoughts, fleeting impressions. Harry Levin has quoted a passage from Fanny Burney's diary which asks "demurely for comparison with the last words of Molly Bloom," but diaries—like letters—tend on the whole to be as organized as soliloquies. Wyndham Lewis, an early critic of the Joycean technique, drew our attention to some of the staccato accents of Alfred Jingle, Esq., in the *Pickwick Papers* and asked us to compare them with those of Leopold Bloom's mind:

Terrible place—dangerous work—other day—five children —mother—tall lady, eating sandwiches—forgot the arch— crash—knock—children look round—mother's head off— sandwich in her hand—no mouth to put it in—head of a family off—shocking, shocking. Looking at Whitehall, Sir—fine place —little window—somebody's else's head off there, eh, sir?—he didn't keep a sharp look-out enough either—eh, Sir, eh?

It is quite obvious that one can exhume endless passages from the literature of the past which resemble the contemporary stream of consciousness or internal monologue. But to do so is perhaps to dismiss too airily the deeper meaning for the novel of our time of this "inward-turning" of a whole group of twentieth-century artists.

3

From the first, the novelists of the past were aware that they could not hope to report to us as circumstantially on mental data as they could on the physical data of our world. "These words represent in brief the thousand and one thoughts which floated through his mind," Balzac wrote of Eugène de Rastignac, and we have the spectacle of a greater master of fictional detail contenting himself with a mere digest from the moment he seeks to deal with subjective material. Henry James, at nineteen, when he wrote an anonymously published story, was precociously careful to distinguish between action, which he could describe with Defoesque verisimilitude, and thoughts which belonged to someone else—and which the author, theoretically, could not adequately possess:

> Though I have judged best, hitherto, often from an exaggerated fear of trenching on the ground of fiction, to tell you what this poor lady did and said, rather than what she thought, I may disclose what passed in her mind now.

Dostoevsky, in one of his tales, stated the problem implied in Balzac's sentence with the utmost clarity:

> It is well known that whole trains of thought sometimes pass through our brains instantaneously, as though they were sensations, without being translated into human speech, still less into a literary language. But we will try to translate these sensations of our hero's, and present to the reader at least the kernel of them, so to say, what was most essential and nearest to reality in them. For many of our sensations when translated into ordinary language seem absolutely unreal. That is why they never find expression, though everyone has them.

The novelists of the nineteenth century thus agreed that subjective states could be *reported* but not *rendered* in the novel. And William James's brilliant account of the psychology of thought in his *Principles of Psychology* of 1890 offered a striking confirmation of this view. It was William James who named the "stream of consciousness"; the metaphor was invoked by him to describe the flux of the mind, its continuity and yet its continuous change.

Consciousness, William James said, is an amalgam of all that we have experienced and continue to experience. Every thought is a part of a personal consciousness; every thought is also unique and ever-changing. We seem to be selective in our thoughts, selectively attentive or inattentive, focusing attention on certain objects and areas of experience, rejecting others, totally blocking others out.

When a thought recurs in the mind it can never be exactly the same as it was before. Renewed, it carries with it the freshness of renewal, and the new context in which it has re-emerged. "Experience is remoulding us every moment, and our mental reaction on every given thing is really a resultant of our experience of the whole world up to that date." This is true not only for ideas, but for our sensory perceptions as the consciousness registers them.

Thought has changes of pace. It involves a "clearly lighted centre of experience" surrounded by a twilight region—a "fringe" or "halo" of other thoughts. What is important for us above all, however, is William James's description of the difficulty of catching the thoughts in their flow, of arresting them and examining them.

The rush of thought is so headlong that it almost always brings us up at the conclusion before we can arrest it. Or if our purpose is nimble enough and we do arrest it, it ceases forthwith to be itself. As a snowflake crystal caught in the warm hand is no longer a crystal but a drop, so, instead of catching the feeling of relation moving to its term, we find we have caught some substantive thing, usually the last word we were pronouncing, statically taken, and with its function, tendency, and particular meaning in the sentence quite evaporated. The attempt at introspective analysis in these cases is in fact like seizing a spinning top to catch its motion, or trying to turn up the gas quickly enough to see how the darkness looks.

Does this mean that the novelist, in seeking to write of what goes on in the mind, attempts the impossible? Is he foredoomed to continual frustration in his attempt to put consciousness into words, to find always there is light instead of darkness when he seeks to turn his light upon the darkness, or that the snowflake turns to water even as he holds it in his hand? Is there no way in which to seize the spinning top and to keep it spinning at the same time?

How render in prose fiction our immediate perception of the world around us, the multitude of direct impressions and the "fringes" and "haloes" of thought, conscious and unconscious, that surround them while, say, we are delivering a reasonably straight sentence to a friend seated opposite us at a table? We may note the details of his face as we talk, its expression, its colouring, or the colour of his attire, or the shape of his necktie, or the wart on his neck; the distinctive aspects may float into the clearly lighted centre of our experience or remain on the fringe, while we are aware of thinking about what we are saying and at the same time an active fantasy is playing through our mind on still another level that may reflect the feelings we have about the person opposite us, or may wander away entirely from the scene to field and sea, or other faces, or a game of golf, even while we still coherently address the man and even while our eyes catch his expression and register it and our ears record his laughter, his words, the noise of a passing car, a distant train whistle, the clatter of dishes, the girl three tables away putting on lipstick; and at the same time we raise automatically the cup of coffee to our lips, aware of its taste (even to noting the components, say, the amount of sugar we have put in) and its temperature, and if we are inclined to Proustian association, the sip may evoke other coffee-drinkings that in turn flood our memory as if it were a flickering cinema that pulls together images and words; and through all this the talk is sustained and the figure opposite is unaware of the richness of our multitudinous impressions—as we are unaware of its impressions, save those it will articulate.

This quite organized attempt on my part to indicate the simultaneity of mental experience can be only a skeleton-diagram of consciousness. It cannot begin to convey the complexity of thought and of sensory experience. How record, word by word, such symphonic material, in which certain instruments often speak out but in which, around them, the voices of others are constantly breaking in? How keep the core of thought disengaged from the haloes and fringes? It cannot be done, and if it could it would tax our reading attention far beyond its capacity. The result, in any event, would be of as dubious artistic value as a gramophone record of the noises in the restaurant.

We recognize, therefore, that Balzac and Dostoevsky

were right when they spoke of the need to digest the thoughts of their characters and of *translating* sensations into words. What they could not have taken into account at that time was the possibility of the artist's creating the *illusion* that we are inside the mind of the character by the same process through which, say, Balzac creates the illusion that we are inside the Maison Vauquer: by the massing of detail in such a way that the interior comes alive, so that we feel ourselves within the boarding-house and among its people as the story unfolds. Or, what the nineteenth-century writers could not foresee, that an interior such as the Dedalus home at Christmas could be re-created not by the massing of the realistic physical detail, but by making real for us the intense emotions within that household. The critics in the 1920s took a wrong turning (later amply rectified) when they said that James Joyce had not accurately given us the thoughts of his characters in *Ulysses*. They spoke as if Joyce had turned a motion-picture camera into the minds of Stephen and Leopold and Molly and was supposed to convey to us everything that it found there. Even so thoughtful a practitioner of the craft of fiction as Edith Wharton described stream-of-consciousness writing as the recording of the "unsorted abundance" of thought and impression. These critics failed to understand that Joyce was exercising close selection and arrangement even when he seemed to dredge up a great deal of unrelated associational matter. His selection was addressed to the creating of an illusion *that there had been no selection.* For Joyce was aware that his was an act of *translating* into words material that by its evanescence defied verbal description. He knew, in other words, the lessons of the symbolist movement.

4

We return to old ground, we are back among the symbolists and their revolt against naturalism. We are also back in the 1880s, again listening to the famous debate on the novel between Walter Besant and Henry James, with Robert Louis Stevenson eloquently chiming in. It was Stevenson who joined the issue with great clarity:

Life is monstrous, infinite, illogical, abrupt and poignant; a work of art, in comparison, is neat, finite, self-contained, rational, flowing and emasculate. Life imposes by brute energy, like inarticulate thunder; art catches the ear, among the far louder noises of experience, like an air artificially made by a discreet musician. . . . The novel, which is a work of art, exists, not by its resemblances to life, which are forced and material, as a shoe must still consist of leather, but by its immeasurable difference from life, which is designed and significant, and is both the method and the meaning of the work.

Substitute the word "thought" or "perceptual experience" for "life" in this striking passage, and Stevenson's remarks would apply with equal force to the novel of subjectivity.

In this same debate, Henry James extended the definition of experience and the province of fiction to include the subjective world:

Humanity is immense, and reality has a myriad forms; the most one can affirm is that some of the flowers of fiction have the odour of it, and others have not; as for telling you in advance how your nosegay should be composed, that is another affair. It is equally excellent and inconclusive to say that one must write from experience; to our supposititious aspirant such a declaration might savour of mockery. What kind of experience is intended, and where does it begin and end? Experience is never limited, and it is never complete; it is an immense sensibility, a kind of huge spider-web of the finest silken threads suspended in the chamber of consciousness, and catching every airborne particle in its tissue. It is the very atmosphere of the mind; and when the mind is imaginative—much more when it happens to be that of a man of genius—it takes to itself the faintest hints of life, it converts the very pulses of the air into revelations.

Atmosphere of the mind. This is a very happy phrase. It comes closer to describing—in so far as it is describable— what the writers of novels dealing with the subjective life of their characters have tried to do. Whether they seek to render mental experience through one or another of the techniques that have been devised—and the writers have been extremely inventive in discovering new ones—or resort simply to the first-person self-analysis of Proust, they are invariably trying to capture for the reader the atmosphere of the mind.

From the moment they do so, certain important problems arise, involving the relationship between the writer and his characters and the writer and the reader. For the writer there is the initial problem of the *kind* of mind he will select. It is obvious that the duller the mind, the more resourceful he will have to be in maintaining the interest of the reader. Once he has made this choice he must face a second problem: the writer must in some way disengage himself from his character. The thoughts, whether stream of consciousness or internal monologue, must speak for themselves without his intervening as narrator. This is not as new a problem as it might seem. "The artist ought to be in his work like God in creation, invisible, and all-powerful; let him be felt everywhere but not seen," wrote Flaubert long ago. Taine's image was that of the artist cutting the umbilical cord that bound him to his work. Joyce, facing this problem in writing his subjective fiction, was echoing Flaubert when he described the dramatic artist as one who, "like the God of the creation, remains within or behind or beyond or above his handiwork . . . paring his fingernails." And this raises the further question—it will deserve a whole chapter to itself—whether an artist drawing upon the contents of his own mind (which is the only mind he can use in his creation) is really able to detach himself from his characters: that is whether their subjectivity is not, in reality, *his* subjectivity. In other words: is not a subjective novel but a disguised form of autobiography? To this Proust offers us a definitive answer, as we shall see.

Difficult as these problems are, there remains perhaps the most difficult of all. Once the attempt is made to render a certain mind, there ensues the meeting of that mind with the mind of the reader. There can follow a merging of the two mental atmospheres. In the old novels this was not the case. The reader was being told a story. He listened. He was drawn into it primarily through identification with one or another of the characters. In the modern psychological novel there is no "story" in the old sense, and there is only one character (at a time) with which to identify onself. If the author succeeds in drawing the reader into this single consciousness, he should be able to make the reader *feel* with the character: and the reader does this only if proper identification with the character is achieved. He may then hear the same sounds of Dublin Bloom hears, or feel the sea-shells crunching underfoot as he walks not only with but *as* Dedalus on the beach; or pause to hear the bronze tones of Big Ben as Mrs Dalloway, or allow his own smell-memory to come into play when Benjy, in *The Sound and the Fury*, tells him that Caddy smelled like trees or that Versh smelled like rain. The entire Benjy section reads like the opening paragraphs of *A Portrait of the Artist as a Young Man*. We are in the mind here, however, of a mentally retarded individual who has been "three years old thirty years." And it is Faulkner's achievement to have made Benjy real for us even when we cannot wholly identify ourselves with him, by making us aware of the poetry of the idiot mind and provoking in us compassion and sympathy. He has at the same time manœuvred us into the double position of reading on Benjy's childish level of awareness—as a direct experience—while exercising our own adult capacities to make sense out of the data furnished by Benjy's mind. There is, in other words, the story that is told by the flowing thoughts of Benjy—and the story to be deduced from them by the reader.

What is remarkable about a novel such as *Ulysses*, or the Faulkner novel of which we have been speaking, is that by the time we have finished reading it we have visited—indeed we have lived inside—the minds of several persons. This we cannot do in our everyday life, where we are shut up in only one consciousness—our own. By this process of involving us directly in the mental experience of the characters, the psychological novel has added a significant dimension to the art of prose fiction. To read such a novel can be as never before an enlargement of our own experience. The old-time reader of novels sat down with his book and made a simple demand upon the author: "Beguile me, offer me comedy and tears, tell me about droll people and lovers, and a story that will keep me rooted to the spot and my eyes glued to the page." The case is reversed when we come to the subjective novel. It is the author who says to the reader: "Here is the artistic record of a mind, at the very moment that it is thinking. Try to penetrate within it. You will know only as much as this mind may reveal. It is you, not I, who will piece together any 'story' there may be. Of course I have arranged this illusion for you. But it is you who must experience it."

CHAPTER II

THE INWARD TURNING

IT WAS in reality no coincidence that Marcel Proust, James Joyce, and Dorothy Richardson found themselves writing psychological novels at the century's turn. They were children of the romantic century: rationalism and reason had long before yielded to introspection and feeling. If classicism was intellect and repose, romanticism was self-absorption and flux. The romantic hero began by contemplating his heart; he ended by contemplating his mind. And he discovered that heart, symbol of feeling and perception, and mind, symbol of thought and reason, could be closely related. Often the mind tried to explain away that which the heart felt.

The psychological novel, accidentally founded by Samuel Richardson, by the use of an epistolary method that brought the reader close to the thoughts and feelings of his characters, had given way to the self-conscious modern psychological novel, in which the thoughts and feelings themselves were re-created. Coleridge described Samuel Richardson as recording "the morbid consciousness of every thought and feeling in the whole flux and reflux of the mind, in short its self-involution and dreamlike continuity." Criticism is never more fertile than when, in assessing the past, it sees into the future. Coleridge, in writing of "the flux and reflux of the mind," was in reality describing what the stream-of-consciousness novel would attempt to do. It was he who spoke also of the "twilight reaches of consciousness" and the "modes of inmost being" in describing the "willing suspension of disbelief" which every writer asks of his reader. Maupassant expressed the same thought when he wrote: "*Faire vrai consiste . . . à donner l'illusion complète du vrai . . . les Réalistes de talent devraient s'appeler plutôt des Illusionnistes.*"

27

And Baudelaire spoke of "suggestive magic" as being the function of "pure art," which Jules Laforgue re-expressed when he wrote that "the work of art can never be the equivalent of fugitive reality." If the symbolists, and the naturalists against whom they revolted, regarded themselves as irreconcilable, the two had, at bottom, similar ends in view. The naturalist might cling to his weighty documents and the symbolist to his symbols: both, however, wanted to create an *illusion* of reality.

The modern psychological novel is "modern" in that it reflects the deeper and more searching *inwardness* of our century, and this turning inward was reflected in the writings of William James and Henri Bergson and after them, on the experimental and clinical level, in the work of Sigmund Freud. Their exploration of the psychology of thought—of consciousness—went far beyond the close analysis of it such as Hume and Locke, Berkeley and Mill had courageously attempted. When Proust, Joyce, and Dorothy Richardson began to write, the influence of Freud was only beginning to be felt; and it is to Bergson, in his influence on Proust (and to some extent on Joyce), and to William James, in his account of thought-experience, that we must look as the creators of the intellectual atmosphere in which the novel of subjectivity came into being. As has often been the case, changes in philosophical thought heralded technical innovations in the arts.

We know that Proust studied briefly under Bergson and that he read his works. He mentions him only once, in *Cities of the Plain*, in connection with the effects of soporific drugs on memory. Memory, however, is at the heart of Bergson's explorations, as it is of Proust's. Bergson's concept of time—*la durée*—as the measure of existence, "the invisible progress of the past, which gnaws into the future," his thesis of the use of the past in the evolution of the creative act, his discussions of intuition and reality, his belief in the flux of experience—all these ideas are taken up and studied with extraordinary refinement by Proust. Like William James, Bergson taught that we are remoulded constantly by experience; that consciousness is a process of endless accretion, so long as mind and senses are functioning; that it is "the continuation of an indefinite past in a living present." And out of this comes also the preoccupation with time which is central to the psychological novel. The watch measures off the hours with continuing regularity, but consciousness sometimes makes an hour seem like a day or a day like an hour. In the mind past and present merge: we suddenly call up a memory of childhood that is chronologically of the distant past; but in it memory becomes instantly vivid and is relived for the moment that it is recalled. So, in setting down in the novel the thoughts as they are passing through the mind of the character, the novelist is catching and recording the present moment—and no other. It was no accident that Joyce sought to record a single day in *Ulysses* and that throughout Virginia Woolf there is a preoccupation with "the moment."

It would be wrong, however, to attach Proust solely to Bergson. In Bergson he found certain important—and congenial—philosophical and psychological ideas; to give them expression, artistically, he turned to the literary movement that was at its height when he came to maturity. For Proust had learned much from the symbolists; and what they believed—on an artistic level—came very close to Bergsonism. Bergson described the flux of life. They sought to capture it in words. The evanescence of experience, they held, could be evoked in literature only through the use of images and symbols—the personal symbols of a given artist. It required the verbal beauty of the mind to express the mind. "My keyboard is perpetually changing," wrote Laforgue, "and there is no other keyboard which is identical with mine." The roots of Proust's novel reach deeply into the symbolist movement.

What of Joyce?

In as complex a figure, nourished on Aquinas and on Vico, aware of the literary movements of his time and able to draw upon many literatures by virtue of his great linguistic gifts, we must expect to find a meeting of many sources. These have been described and dealt with in great detail by the many critics of the Irish writer, and doubtless much remains to be explored. But there is one

29

source which primarily concerns us in the present inquiry. It was widely proclaimed by Joyce himself, yet it has not been taken seriously enough. In his twentieth year, James Joyce read a French novel of 1888—written at the height of the symbolist ferment. It was by Édouard Dujardin and was titled *Les lauriers sont coupés*. George Moore had talked about it in Dublin and about its author, who was his friend. Joyce appears to have been profoundly impressed by its narrative technique. From the first word to the last, the reader found himself inside the mind of the principal character. Very little actually happens in the book. A young man-about-town in Paris is in love with an actress. She asks him constantly for money; this he gives to her in the hope that ultimately she will bestow upon him more than sweet words and a smile. His hopes turn out to be ill founded. It is, as fiction, a pretty small affair. One would hardly think it capable of influencing, even in remote fashion, so largely-proportioned a work as *Ulysses*. Yet Joyce, when asked where his stream-of-consciousness technique stemmed from always announced his debt to Édouard Dujardin. Dujardin was then still alive although his novel had been long forgotten. The French writer promptly likened himself to Lazarus rising from the dead—and indeed he was a living author who had gained a glimpse of his posthumous reputation. Joyce proclaimed his debt to Dujardin, Dujardin proclaimed *his* debt to Joyce. The present had exalted the past. *Les lauriers sont coupés* was reprinted with a Preface by Valéry Larbaud, the French critic who first explained the Homeric structure of *Ulysses*. The book was reviewed as if it were a new work, and its method of narration was baptized *post factum* by Larbaud as *le monologue intérieur*. In a lecture delivered in 1930, Dujardin sought to define internal monologue and attributed to Paul Bourget the first use of the term. While it is interesting to think of Bourget, with his passion for what passed as "psychology" in his time, as the originator of the term, the credit for its application to the subjective or stream-of-consciousness novel really belongs to Larbaud.

Mary Colum, in her reminiscences, claims that Joyce's

resuscitation of the Dujardin novel was a hoax, an elaborately embroidered Joycean joke. If she is right it was a cruel joke perpetrated upon an elderly and much-respected man of letters—and one taken much too seriously by the literary world to be funny. A reading of the Dujardin novel, however, supplies the answer and can set our mind at rest. Faded and distant it is, but it is without a doubt the first consistently sustained (even though technically primitive) stream-of-consciousness novel to have been published.

It is not difficult to see today how Joyce took the measure of Dujardin's experiment, saw what was of value in it, and built upon it with the extraordinary verbal skill which made it possible for him to succeed where Dujardin failed. In acknowledging his debt to Dujardin, Joyce, by implication, acknowledged his debt to the French symbolist movement, for Dujardin was of the symbolists, and his work sprang directly from the Tuesdays at Mallarmé's and the literary ferment in the Paris of the 1880s.

Edmund Wilson long ago defined the relationship between the symbolists and the work of Joyce and Proust, in his admirable study, *Axel's Castle*. In that volume he distilled from the elaborate theorizing of the French poets the essence of symbolist doctrine as follows:

Every feeling or sensation we have, every moment of consciousness, is different from every other; and it is, in consequence, impossible to render our sensations as we actually experience them through the conventional and universal language of ordinary literature. Each poet has his unique personality; each of his moments has its special tone, its special combination of elements. And it is the poet's task to find, to invent, the special language which will alone be capable of expressing his personality and feelings.

This, in effect, is what the symbolists sought to do, and in Joyce there was to be the strange and rewarding—and paradoxical—spectacle of a supreme realist, in the tradition of both Flaubert and Zola, turning to the methods of the symbolists to achieve his realism. When it was published, the Dujardin novel (as might be expected)

31

attracted very little attention. However, Rémy de Gourmont recognized its qualities. He described it as "a novel which seems in literature a transposed anticipation of the cinema." George Moore, who corresponded with Dujardin, read the book during its serialization in *La Revue Indépendante* and wrote to him that it revealed for the first time "the inner life of the soul." He added *"seulement je crains la monotonie. Nous verrons; en tout cas, c'est neuf."* Moore's fear that the method might prove monotonous pointed to one of its possible shortcomings. That, however, remained to be discovered.

2

If Proust and Joyce stemmed from the enveloping climate of introspection and subjectivity—in reality the continued flowering of romanticism—in the late nineteenth century, with certain significant points of attachment to the symbolists, what impulse set Dorothy Richardson on her elaborate fictional experiment? Readers who asked this question found no direct answer. There was no doubt that if Miss Richardson's succeeding volumes did appear to reach a dead level of monotony for some, she was nevertheless faithfully adhering to her method. By the time the eighth volume—or chapter—had appeared, in 1925 (*The Trap*), readers knew little more about the "hard" facts of Miriam Henderson's life than they had discovered in the first volume. They knew, however, a great deal about her moods and her feelings and the quality of her mind; and they remained sealed in the envelope of her consciousness. Quite the most remarkable part of Miss Richardson's experiment was her unswerving adherence to the *single* point of view. *The Trap*, however, yielded a highly significant bit of information.

In this portion of *Pilgrimage*, Miriam Henderson is moving into a new apartment. Very early we come upon allusions to a book which has made a profound impression upon the heroine. But she never names it.

Her forgotten book was lying on the table. The book that had suddenly become the centre of her life. . . . She took it in her hands, felt it draw her again with its unique power.

The movers arrive to take her things to the new apartment. She, however, is absorbed by the book.

The men could, must, manage without supervision. For the second time, during which they stood listening as though she had not spoken before, she pointed out the things which were to be taken, and sat down with the book.

She surveys the volume and its letters of gold on a red cover, and remembers how she found it in the subscription library among rows of well-known names of books and writers. (It is a defect in the internal monologue that the title of the book and the name of its author do not once enter the mind of the heroine: and this is difficult to believe, for she fondles the volume and thinks much about it.)

And then this book, for all the neutrality of its title and of the author's name, drawing her hands, bringing, as she took it from the shelf and carried it, unexamined, away down the street, the stillness of contentment.
She could, so long as the men remained, get no further. Within the neat red binding lay the altogether new happiness.

There follow more details of the moving and then we return to the volume:

She glanced through the pages of its opening chapter, the chapter that was now part of her own experience; set down at last alive, so that the few pages stood in her mind, growing as a single good day will grow, in memory, deep and wide, wider than the year to which it belongs. She was surprised to find, coming back after the interval of disturbed days, how little she had read. Just the opening pages, again and again, not wanting to go forward; wanting the presentation of the two men, talking outside time and space in the hotel bedroom, to go on for ever. And presently fearing to read further, lest the perfection of satisfaction should cease.

The identity of the book becomes a charming puzzle for the reader, and there is a kind of teasing perversity in the way in which Miss Richardson feeds us the data: neutral title, neutral name of author, two men talking "outside time and space" in a hotel bedroom. We read on, wondering whether we are to be totally frustrated.

For in Miss Richardson's novel certain thoughts trickle through Miriam's consciousness, never to be explained, never to return—as happens in all minds. There is a remark on the second page of the first volume, "Perhaps Miss Gilkes was right . . ." but we never discover who Miss Gilkes was. Would Miriam reveal the name of this book which she deemed to be so important, or the name of its author? And then:

Reading a paragraph here and there, looking out once more the two phrases that had thrilled her more intimately than any others, she found a stirring of strange statements in her mind. A strange clarity that was threatening to change the adventure of reading to a shared disaster. For she remembered now, having hung for a while over Waymarsh's "sombre glow". . . .

There at last we have it! Waymarsh and Strether in the hotel at Chester. Miriam has in her hands, in the Methuen edition, the red cover with the title stamped in gold, *The Ambassadors*, by Henry James.

This man was a monstrous unilluminated pride. And joy in him was a mark of the same corruption. Pride in discovering the secrets of his technique. Pride in watching it labour with the development of the story. The deep attention demanded by this new way of statement was in itself a self-indulgence. But the cold ignorance of this man was unconscious. And therefore innocent. And it was he after all who had achieved the first completely satisfying way of writing a novel. If this were a novel.

The first completely satisfying way of writing a novel . . . This new way of statement. . . . What had Dorothy Richardson discovered in Henry James that seemed so important to her—or rather to her heroine—so important indeed as to be now "the centre of her life?" The question is worth pursuing.

CHAPTER III

THE POINT OF VIEW

WHAT DíD Dorothy Richardson mean when she spoke of "the first completely satisfying way of writing a novel," as she placed a copy of *The Ambassadors* in the hands of Miriam Henderson? From the few clues she gives us, she seems to have read only as far as Lambert Strether's dinner in London with Maria Gostrey. Yet she discerns in the book, in its first fifty pages, some quality or technique that seems to her—some time before 1910—a "new way of statement."

This new way of statement was Henry James's predilection for maintaining a consistent viewpoint or level of awareness through which the reader is given the facts of his story. He is very careful to explain in the Preface to *The Ambassadors*, written for the New York Edition of his works (not the red-covered first edition read by Miriam), how he has handled his narrative. He might have written a first-person story; but "the first person, in the long piece, is a form foredoomed to looseness." Looseness, he adds, "was never much my affair." His readers, I think, will agree.

What, then, did he do? Instead of allowing his hero, Strether, to reveal himself, his age, his past, his special mission in Europe (as he would in the first person), James sets his ironic comedy into motion in the hotel at Chester: he establishes a play of illumination among three persons. First, Strether, arriving and thinking briefly of the errand that has brought him to Europe, but having no occasion to disclose it; then the chance encounter with Maria Gostrey, who has known Waymarsh and hears Strether speak of him; and finally Waymarsh's arrival. There follows the scene in the hotel room in which Waymarsh attempts to discover from Strether the

35

nature of his special "mission" in Europe, although Strether is clearly in no hurry to talk about it. Finally, the three characters arrive in London after sundry minor adventures of sightseeing and shopping. All the while Strether is receiving impressions and developing more and more a sense of release from the responsibilities and constraints of Woollett, Massachusetts, and Mrs Newsome, who has sent him abroad as her "ambassador."

The "new way of statement" is through a kind of mutual irradiation—Strether illuminating Maria, she illuminating him, both illuminating Waymarsh, and Waymarsh in turn holding up his lamp to look at the other two. It is the method of the drama, the unravelling of an exposition as we get it on the stage, but with the much greater subtlety which a novel permits. Gradually the novel will shift into the mind of Strether, and it is his mind that will light up the whole revelation of Paris and of his task—the initial purpose of which was to rescue Chad Newsome from what Woollett believed was the embrace of a French temptress. Quietly James will hand the kite-string of his story to the reader.

This is what Dorothy Richardson perceived at the time of the novel's publication—and it was perception enough in those days when Henry James's public greeted his books with ever-increasing bewilderment.

2

James called this particular method of revelation of the story, that is illumination of the situation and characters through one or several minds, the *point of view*. Very early in his career he had discovered the trick of making the characters reveal themselves with minimal intervention of the author. But it was not until the writing of his final Prefaces that he fully explained the theories that had guided him. In the very first Preface, discussing the character of Rowland Mallet in *Roderick Hudson*, he tells us that the "centre of interest throughout *Roderick* is in Rowland Mallet's consciousness, and the drama is the very drama of that consciousness." He goes on to explain that he had to make this consciousness acute but "not *too* acute," for that would have made it superhuman. In other words, "the beautiful little problem was to keep it connected, connected intimately, with the general human exposure, and thereby bedimmed and befooled and bewildered, anxious, restless, fallible, and yet to endow it with such intelligence that the appearances reflected in it, and constituting together there the situation and the 'story,' should become by that fact intelligible." This was the key to the Jamesian method; and Rowland's step-by-step discoveries of the situation before him, and his relation to it, provide an unfolding drama.

In the Preface to *The Portrait of a Lady*—a work he deemed "the most proportioned" of his fictions after *The Ambassadors*—he dwells on what he considered the great scene of that novel, his heroine's review, late one night, of the course her life had taken.

She sits up, by her dying fire, far into the night, under the spell of recognitions on which she finds the last sharpness suddenly wait. It is a representation simply of her motionlessly *seeing*, and an attempt withal to make the mere still lucidity of her act as "interesting" as the surprise of a caravan or the identification of a pirate. It represents, for that matter, one of the identifications dear to the novelist, and even indispensable to him; but it all goes on without her being approached by another person and without her leaving her chair. It is obviously the best thing in the book, but it is only a supreme illustration of the general plan.

The "general plan" in James was to make the reflections of an individual as exciting as an adventure story. James states the plan as if it were a recipe: "Place the centre of the subject in the young woman's own consciousness and you get as interesting and as beautiful a difficulty as you could wish. Stick to *that*—for the centre; put the heaviest weight into *that* scale, which will be so largely the scale of her relation to herself. Make her only interested enough, at the same time, in the things that are not herself, and this relation needn't fear to be too limited. Place meanwhile in the other scale the lighter weight . . . press least hard, in short, on the consciousness of your heroine's satellites, especially the male; make

37

it an interest contributive only to the greater one." James mused that by this means he could produce the "maximum of intensity with the minimum of strain." Isabel's vigil and meditation—it is, in effect, a scrupulously organized and highly sifted internal monologue—is for James a "vigil of searching criticism." The point of view is at the centre of James's aesthetic of the novel. And it must be at the centre of any study of the stream of consciousness in the contemporary novel: for once we are within a given mind we can obviously have only the inner vision, the *point of view* of that particular mind. In studying the problems of his fixed and varying centres of consciousness, Henry James was preparing the way for those who would follow and carry this technique to its logical conclusion: to minor consciousness itself.

3

There are, on the long Jamesian shelf, two pieces of fiction which admirably illustrate the novelist's cunning experiments with the point of view. One of them, *The Turn of the Screw*, has become the subject of a long and rather tiresome controversy arising from a discussion of the circumstantial evidence in the narrative, with the participants, however, failing to examine the technique of the story-telling, which would have made much of the dispute unnecessary. The second has met with general critical bafflement. I refer to *The Sacred Fount*, written in 1900, just before *The Ambassadors*. Two critics, R. P. Blackmur and Edward Sackville-West, have recognized the qualities of art in this short novel, without, however, looking closely at its structure; Edmund Wilson, on the other hand, has understood the structure but has described the novel as "mystifying, even maddening," thereby paying perhaps unintended tribute to Henry James's conscious attempt at "mystification." Other critics, and they are numerous, have either masked their bewilderment in derision or candidly admitted they could not understand. William Dean Howells achieved a rather curious position between the two extremes: he announced, when the book was published, he had mastered its secret, but said he had decided he "wouldn't for the present divulge it." "For the present" lasted seventeen years; thereafter Howells was beyond divulging. Perhaps the most quoted verdict on this novel has been Rebecca West's: that it is "a small, mean story," and that it "worries one like a rat nibbling at the wainscot," a story of how "a week-end visitor spends more intellectual force than Kant can have used on *The Critique of Pure Reason*, in an unsuccessful attempt to discover whether there exists between certain of his fellow-guests a relationship not more interesting among these vacuous people than it is among sparrows."

When criticism throws up its hands in bewilderment over the work of an artist or wavers between such extremes, it is reasonable to inquire whether the work in question is really art. Has there been a failure in communication or a failure in perception—or both? For us the question is pertinent, since in both these works James came closest to creating that type of bewilderment which contemporary novel readers feel at first, say, when they open *The Sound and the Fury* and are plunged into the shifting consciousness of Benjy. Dostoevsky had preceded James in a remarkable story, *Letters from the Underworld*, but there, in the first paragraph, he had semaphored the reader, not with flags but with klieg lights that here was the mind of an eccentric, if not a madman. There is no such obvious signalling in *The Turn of the Screw* or *The Sacred Fount*. In both of these works the reader is led unsuspectingly to accept the narrator in good faith, and this may have been what James meant when he said he had set "a trap for the unwary." In *The Turn of the Screw* James even provides an elaborate testimonial to the good character of the unnamed governess, who is the first-person narrator. Yet in both cases, if the reader reads attentively, he will discover that he is tied down by the limitations James imposes upon him. The data go only so far: beyond, he can have recourse only to his own imagination.

There are, so to speak, three narrators in *The Turn of the Screw*. The first is the individual, perhaps James himself, who begins by telling us, "The story had held us, round the fire. . . ." This unidentified First Narrator goes on to mention a second personage named Douglas. Douglas now briefly takes over the narrative; he tells of a ghost story with a special "turn of the screw." It is related in an old manuscript. Douglas is thus, in a certain sense, Second Narrator, but not technically, since his account is at first being quoted or summarized by the First Narrator. Then, finally, Douglas begins to read the manuscript and the Principal Narrator, the governess, takes over. The story we are finally given is hers, and it is told in the first person. Douglas and the First Narrator disappear, never to return.

Readers often become so wrapped up in the ghosts and the children of *The Turn of the Screw* that they forget this elaborate "frame". In it a great deal of significant information is given to us. Each narrator provides a set of facts, not, however, evaluated for us. We are told the governess has been dead for twenty years. She sent the manuscript to Douglas before she died. Douglas tells us she was ten years older than he was and that she was his sister's governess. "She struck me as awfully clever and nice . . . I liked her extremely." She was twenty when the events described in the manuscript occurred. We are told that forty years have elapsed since her death. Douglas says "it was long ago" that he knew her and "this episode was long before." In fact, he was at Trinity College "and I found her at home on my coming down the second summer." This means that Douglas must have been eighteen or perhaps twenty when he had completed his second year at the university; and the governess, ten years older, would be about thirty when Douglas met her and found her "nice." And the meeting was ten years after the events described in her manuscript.

This is an elaborate and careful time-scheme for James to have set down, and he did so not merely through whim. We know from his working notebooks the care with which he placed every detail in his fictions. The time-scheme is extremely important in this story. It establishes, for one thing, that Douglas's testimony is based on the personality

of the governess as it was ten years *after* the events of the
story. By that time we can presume she had learned the
ways of the world. We are explicitly told that at twenty
she knew little of the world; she had emerged from a
cloistered Hampshire vicarage, the youngest of several
daughters of a poor and—as she describes him—eccentric
country parson. The narrative itself emphasizes her rus-
ticity and unworldliness: she had never seen herself in a
full-length mirror; she had never read a novel (and at Bly
she reads Fielding's *Amelia*, which has the word "rape"
and the word "adultery" on its first page); she has never
seen a play. If we add to these little details the significant
fact that she has received her position from a mysterious
and handsome gentleman in Harley Street who sends her
to Bly to take care of his nephew and niece with only a
maid and an ignorant but well-meaning housekeeper (her
name, Mrs. Grose, suggests her simple-mindedness) for
company, it becomes clear that she has ample reason to be
nervous about the duties and responsibilities conferred on
her. Moreover, she is given *carte blanche*: she must make
her own decisions and may not communicate with her
employer. These are circumstances enough to make for
nervousness and anxiety in a young girl taking her first
job. In effect, she has jumped from a humble parsonage
to the role of mistress of a country house and to vicarious
motherhood of two beautiful children.

What happens thereafter, by her own account, is a story
of her throbbing sense of insecurity and her fanciful
speculations about the governess who preceded her and
the valet with whom that governess was friendly—both of
whom are dead. Her daydreams are filled with the figure
of the man in Harley Street; she takes evening walks hop-
ing to meet him. She encounters instead her first vision
of Peter Quint. He is on the tower; he wears the clothes
of the man in Harley Street; she sees him only from the
waist up.

The governess's account of her stay at Bly is riddled
with inconsistencies which the many critics who have discussed the story have never sufficiently perceived. There
are moments when she is, in a less mad way, doing what

the retired civil servant does in Dostoevsky's *Letters from the Underworld*. She speculates and she assumes—and what she first states as fancy she later states as fact. Most readers have tended to accept her story as "fact" partly because Douglas has given her such a good character at the outset and particularly because of the cunning which James has employed in telling the story.

Let us glance at the second occasion on which the governess sees Quint, that is on the day he appears looking through the window of the dining-room. She does not know that it is Quint, or that he is a ghost. She sees him again from the waist up.

On the spot there came to me the added shock of a certitude that it was not for me he had come there. He had come for someone else.

The flash of this knowledge—for it was knowledge in the midst of dread—produced in me the most extraordinary effect, started, as I stood there, a sudden vibration of duty and courage.

We must remember that we are receiving from the governess her story and *her* interpretation of what she saw or imagined. We are entirely in her mind. She had seen a strange man and she does not at this moment know that he is anything but a palpable man; he resembles the man seen on the tower. But she has the "shock of a certitude" that "it was not for me he had come there." He had come for "someone else." This is to say the least an assumption. But the governess promptly appropriates it as "knowledge in the midst of dread." It is "certitude."

There follows the first vision of the woman, Miss Jessel, or a person the governess believes to be Miss Jessel. She is seen by the governess, or rather *felt*, on the other side of the pond which they have named, in Flora's geography lesson, the Sea of Azof.

I became aware that, on the other side of the Sea of Azof, we had an interested spectator. The way this knowledge gathered in me was the strangest thing in the world--the strangest, that is, except the very much stranger in which it quickly merged itself.

42

She describes how she had sat down with a piece of sewing on a stone bench beside the pond and "in this position I began to take in with certitude, and yet without direct vision, the presence, at a distance, of a third person."

There was no ambiguity in anything; none whatever, at least, in the conviction I from one moment to another found myself forming as to what I should see straight before me and across the lake as a consequence of raising my eyes.

She does not, however, raise her eyes. She continues her sewing in order to steady herself while she is deciding what to do.

She says that while she was sewing she knew "there was an alien object in view" across the pond, and this, she is convinced, is true, even though she tells herself it might be "a messenger, a postman, or a tradesman's boy," one of the men about the place. "That reminder had as little effect on my practical certitude as I was conscious—still even without looking—of its having upon the character and attitude of our visitor. Nothing was more natural than that these things should be the other things they absolutely were not." The young lady, we see, always has an abundance of "certitude." Although she has not yet looked, she would get the "positive identity of the apparition"—she tells herself—"as soon as the small clock of my courage should have ticked out the right second." She has already decided, we see, that it is an apparition. Meanwhile, she glances at little Flora. The girl is ten yards away—we are given the distance—and she expects her to cry out or to show some "sudden innocent sign either of interest or of alarm." It is difficult to understand why, since the child has her back to the water and hence her back to the "visitor" on the other bank. The girl has other things to think of; in her play she is trying to put together two pieces of wood to form a boat.

My apprehension of what she was doing sustained me so that after some seconds I felt I was ready for more. Then I again shifted my eyes—I faced what I had to face.

This is all the evidence we have. And we are at the end of the chapter.

The first paragraph of the next chapter tells us:

I got hold of Mrs. Grose as soon after this as I could; and I
can give no intelligible account of how I fought out the interval.
Yet I still hear myself cry as I fairly threw myself into her arms:
"They *know*—it's too monstrous: they know, they know!"

Mrs Grose, naturally, wants to know what they know.
"Why, all that *we* know—and heaven knows what else
besides!" And she adds, "Two hours ago, in the garden
. . . Flora *saw*!"

A supposition has now become a fact, for this is clearly
not what the governess previously described. Her own
fancy has quite carried her away. After telling us that
Flora had her back to the Sea of Azof and was preoccupied with two pieces of wood, she nevertheless tells Mrs
Grose that the girl *saw* what was on the other shore.

Mrs Grose, true to her name, is down to earth about
such matters. "She has told you?" she asks.

"Not a word—that's the horror. She kept it to herself!
The child of eight, *that* child!"

Mrs Grose persists. Her logic is sound enough: "Then
how do you know?"

"I was there—I saw with my eyes: saw that she was
perfectly aware." This is a significant shift of ground—
from *seeing* to her knowledge of *awareness*. She then tells
Mrs Grose that she saw across the pond a woman who was
Miss Jessel.

"How can you be sure?" Mrs Grose asks.

The governess says: "Then ask Flora—*she's* sure!"

But she has an afterthought. "I had no sooner spoken
than I caught myself up. 'No, for God's sake, *don't*!
She'll say she isn't—she'll lie!' "

Mrs Grose rebels at this. "Ah, how *can* you?"

"Because I'm clear. Flora doesn't want me to know."

"It's only then to spare you."

"No, no—there are depths, depths! The more I go
over it, the more I see in it, and the more I see in it the
more I fear. I don't know what I *don't* see—what I *don't*
fear!"

The governess's imagination, we see, discovers "depths"

44

within herself. Fantasy seems to be reality for her. Anything and everything can and does happen, in her mind. The attentive reader, when he is reading the story critically, can only observe that we are always in the realm of the supposititious. Not once in the entire story do the children see anything strange or frightening. It is the governess's theory that they see as much as she does, and that they communicate with the dead. But it is the governess who does all the seeing and all the supposing. "My values are positively all blanks save only so far as an excited horror, a promoted pity, a created expertness," James explained in his Preface. But we have one significant clue to the author's "blanks." In his revision of the story for the New York Edition he altered his text again and again to put the story into the realm of the governess's feelings. Where he had her say originally "I saw" or "I believed" he often substituted "I felt."

We have here thus in reality two stories, and a method that foreshadows the problems of the stream-of-consciousness writer. One is the area of fact, the other the area of fancy. There is the witness, in this case the governess and her seemingly circumstantial story, and there is the mind itself, the contents of which are given to the reader. The reader must establish for himself the credibility of the witness; he must decide between what the governess *supposed* and what she claims she saw. Read in this fashion, *The Turn of the Screw* becomes an absorbing study of a troubled young woman, with little knowledge or understanding of children, called upon to assume serious responsibilities for the first time in her life. She finds support for her own lack of assurance by telling herself she is courageous and "wonderful." Yet in reality and by her own admission, she is filled with endless fears: "I don't know what I *don't* see—and what I *don't* fear!" The life she describes at Bly is serene enough outwardly: the servants are obedient and devoted to their master and the children. The children are on the whole well behaved at Bly—and sufficiently normal to indulge in a measure of mischief. It is the governess who sees ghosts and reads sinister meanings into everything around her. It is she who subjects the children to a psychological harassment that in the end leads to Flora's hysteria and Miles's death.

In the controversies that have raged about this work, certain critics have argued that James was telling us a ghost story pure and simple, and that there *are* ghosts in the tale, and that to attempt to explain the governess is to be "over-rationalistic." The ghosts, of course, are there: they belong to the experience of the governess. But to attempt to dismiss any weightier critical consideration of the tale on grounds of too much "rationalism" is to overlook the art of the narrator. Regardless of what any clinical diagnosis of the governess might be, or any judgment of her credibility as a witness, there remains her sense of horror and the extent to which it is communicated to the reader. And it is because there is this question of her feeling, and its communication to the reader, that there has been so much critical argument: for each reader feels the story differently and fills in the Jamesian blanks in accordance with these feelings. In describing Balzac's Valérie Marneffe, James spoke of the French novelist's giving her "the long rope, for her acting herself out." The governess acts herself out, that is the essence of the art used in this story. As in the case of Isabel Archer, we are made aware of her "relation to herself." And by this, *The Turn of the Screw* foreshadows the psychological fiction of our century.

4

The Sacred Fount has never found the wide public of *The Turn of the Screw*, and doubtless never will. For in it the narrator, in whose mind we find ourselves from beginning to end, neither engages our sympathy nor indulges in an inquiry as absorbing as the inquiry of the governess at Bly. Here there is no prelude, no attempt to give us a setting for the story or a certain amount of data about the narrator. The reader is helpless from the start: he is confined exclusively to the evidence furnished by the one mind.

The story itself, as told to us by this unnamed man (it becomes clear early that he is a man), is an account of a

46

fantastic attempt to worm out a series of relationships among the guests at a week-end party at a place called Newmarch. The narrator is led to believe that in the case of one couple there is physical depletion of the younger husband by his older wife. The husband has aged rapidly. It seems to the narrator, therefore, that she is becoming younger at her spouse's expense. And with his fondness for parallel situations, James creates also a man, hitherto foolish, who has now grown wise. The narrator's logical mind promptly translates this observation into a neat problem: whose "sacred fount" is this individual draining in the process of acquiring his superior mental capacities? The answer, obviously, is to look for a woman depleted of her wit.

And so this haunted and morbid tale plays itself out as a kind of mental detective story which is also a species of mental keyhole-peeping on the part of the narrator. He seeks to understand the relationships of the people around him, about which he has such curious hypotheses, and the reader is helpless—if he persists to the end—for he is caught in the trap of the narrator's calculations and conclusions. But what of the credibility of the witness? One of the characters in the story, toward the end, says to him: "You're abused by a fine fancy." Again: "You build up houses of cards." Again: ". . . You over-estimate the penetration of others." Finally, point-blank: "I think you're crazy." Some readers are inclined to agree.

This short novel of Henry James's seems to be almost a *reductio ad absurdum* of the point-of-view method. Certainly it suggests the limits beyond which a novelist may not go in presenting to the reader a character's "relation" to himself. At a given moment the narrator wonders whether it is right "to nose about for a relation that a lady has her reasons for keeping secret." The fellow-visitor, an artist, to whom he makes the remark, reassures him that this can be harmless, and even "positively honourable" so long as the investigator adheres to "psychological evidence." He observes that "resting on psychologic signs alone, it's a high application of the intelligence. What's ignoble," he adds, "is the detective and the keyhole."

47

The narrator accepts this gratifying rationalisation and pursues his researches as a "high application of the intelligence." But he has his moments of serious doubt. Is he not the victim of a "ridiculous obsession"? He has meditated on the danger of seeking "a law that would fit certain given facts." And he warns himself against grouping these facts "into a larger mystery . . . than the facts, as observed, yet warranted." As he watches the guests at dinner he feels himself "seriously warned . . . not to yield further to my idle habit of reading into mere human things an interest so much deeper than mere human things were in general prepared to supply." Yet he is vain of his faculties of observation and insight. "*I* alone was magnificently and absurdly aware—everyone else was benightedly out of it." One of the guests warns him: "Give up . . . the attempt to be a providence. . . . A real providence *knows*; whereas you . . . have to find out." Her warning falls on deaf ears. The narrator congratulates himself on his "supernatural acuteness," his "plunges of insight," his "intellectual mastery" and the joy "of determining, almost of creating results!"

Almost creating results! Then he does think himself a providence! He describes himself, toward the end of the week-end, as having created a veritable "palace of thought." What he discovers, however, is that it is a collapsing house of cards. For, point by point, one of the guests opposes obvious answers to his intricate solutions. The lady tells him "people have such a notion of what you embroider on things that they're rather afraid to commit themselves or to lead you on." In other words, even the testimony he accumulated in talk with others is suspect. "You're costing me a perfect palace of thought," he mourns. There is nothing he can do. She seems to oppose to his ornate speculations only blunt realities. "I *should* certainly never again, on the spot, quite hang together, even though it wasn't really that I hadn't three times her method. What I too fatally lacked was her tone." With these words Henry James rings down the indecisive curtain on his narrator. Nothing has been solved, nothing settled. The reader can only take the narrator at his ambiguous word. The narrator has combined his curiosity with the *savoir faire* of a man of the world who also has the sensitivity of the artist. We have discovered he is addicted to gossip and to the intellectualizing of every human situation; he seems to be prey to anxieties unless he can achieve a kind of intellectual superiority and omniscience over those around him. It is this which makes him feel secure. He is kind, sympathetic, romantic, solitary, proud—and persistent in his curiosity. All this we can deduce. While it may be a great deal, in terms of the narrator's personality, it tells us nothing about the everyday facts of his life. What is his name? What does he look like? What does he do when he isn't "nosing about" to determine a lady's secret? As was the case with the governess of *The Turn of the Screw*, we know nothing more than the person involved has told us in the process of "acting himself out." This is what Henry James meant when he wrote to H. G. Wells he had to keep the governess "impersonal." More impersonal even than the governess is the narrator of *The Sacred Fount*.

What world are we in when we have wandered into that strange week-end at Newmarch and found ourselves totally at the mercy of the narrator, limited exclusively to his vision as we were to the governess's vision of Bly? These two works are not isolated on the long shelf of Henry James's fiction. From 1896 to the century's turn he wrote a series of studies of persons seeking to fathom the world around them, and so arranged the telling of the stories that the reader must actively fathom it with them. This is the method of the drama: it is also the method of the traditional detective story. The works follow in a logical progression: *What Maisie Knew*, in which the reader must determine how much a "light vessel of consciousness," a little girl, knew of the world of divorce and adultery into which she was thrown; *The Turn of the Screw*, with the governess seeking to fathom the world at Bly largely created by herself; the little telegraph girl of *In the Cage*, piecing together from her limited angle of vision the meanings of the messages she dispatches in her capacity as clerk in a telegraph office; *The Awkward Age*, in which the heroine, emerging from late adolescence, tries to put together the meaning of the adult world into which her mother prematurely thrusts her; and finally, *The Sacred Fount*. James admitted that these characters all possess a "rage of wonderment." The reader must acquire the same "rage," for in each case, with the exception of *The Awkward Age*, we remain largely within the given "point of view." The reader's mind is forced to hold to two levels of awareness: *the story as told*, and *the story to be deduced*. This is the calculated risk Henry James took in writing for audiences not prepared to read him so actively. The writer of stream of consciousness takes the same risk.

5

In locating his angle of vision in one specific consciousness, or in a series of reflecting minds, James anticipated most of the problems of the stream-of-consciousness writers. One more step was needed: this was the creation of the illusion that the reader actually follows the character's flowing thought. There are moments in James— *The Jolly Corner* comes to mind—when he has virtually written a kind of internal monologue. In his work, however, he not only selects the thoughts, analysing them at times in a manner that foreshadows Proust, but he is deeply concerned over the kind of consciousness he will present to the reader. There was no merit, James argued, in mirroring the consciousness of the "headlong fools" of this world. In a long work it was necessary to find an illuminating intelligence, capable of contributing the greatest interest and the deepest understanding of the life the author wished to re-create. Such an intelligence becomes a sensitive register, a receptacle of the lucidity to be imparted to the reader. The novelist, however, did not rule out the interest for fiction of a more limited intelligence in a given case, and he warned against "filling too full any supposed and above all limited vessel of consciousness."

Concretely James saw that the psychological novelist is

primarily concerned with "what a man thinks and what he feels." These constituted, he wrote, "the history and the character of what he does." "The figures in any picture," said James, "the agents in any drama, are interesting only in proportion as they feel their respective situations." With that need for fine distinction, he discussed the different degrees of feeling: the muffled and the faint, the just-sufficient, the "barely intelligent," as against "the acute, the intense, the complete." For the "*leading* interest" in a novel James preferred a "finely aware" character—aware as Hamlet was, or Lear. His invocation of Hamlet and Lear might give us pause. Was not James adapting a very old concept to his contemporary world? The old dramatists chose the struggles and conflicts of kings and queens for their subjects, since the essence of classical tragedy was the fall of a person of high estate. James sought to create superior minds to give his dramas nobler themes, finer substance, higher tension. For him there had to be—in a large work—a "consciousness subject to fine intensification and wide enlargement. It is as mirrored in that consciousness that the gross fools, the headlong fools, the fatal fools play their part for us—they have much less to show us in themselves."

Some critics have fallen into the habit of saying that James ruled out the "fools" of this world from his fiction save as reflected elements of life. This, of course, is to mis-read what he said; moreover, there are fools in abundance in his work. It is important for us to understand that James was expressing a preference for an illuminating intelligence as a "*leading* interest"—the italic was his —"at the centre of our subject." Elsewhere in the same passage he very clearly says "I think no 'story' is possible without its fools."

The generalization for the contemporary psychological novelist in this careful Jamesian theorizing may be stated as follows: from the moment we are inside the mind of a character we are committed to that character's *point of view*. It follows that the more intense the perceiver, the more intense the experience of the reader. The writer must be aware of the limits of the consciousness he is projecting: he must not make a limited mind too perceptive, nor impose limitations where there is abundant capacity for perception. Each consciousness, in other words, must be kept consistent within itself. Faulkner's Benjy is an admirable illustration of the careful observance of James's admonitions.

CHAPTER IV

THE INTERNAL MONOLOGUE

WE HAVE seen how difficult it is for the novelist to set down in words a record of inner experience. It has been no less difficult for criticism to find adequate terms to describe this literary process. William James chose the metaphor "stream of consciousness" only after discarding "chain of thought" and "train of thought"—both phrases seeming to him to suggest too much the idea that thought is jointed. "A 'river' or a 'stream' are the metaphors by which it is most naturally described," he wrote. "In talking of it hereafter, let us call it the stream of thought, of consciousness or of subjective life." Since the writing of these words, criticism has fumbled without success for an adequate, all-inclusive label. A series of "interior" labels was devised: interior vision, interior cinema, interior or internal monologue—and it is the latter which has acquired considerable currency. (James Joyce, with his characteristic genius for adding a wry verbal twist to such phrases, turns it, in *Finnegans Wake*, into "the steady monologuy of the interiors.")

When Joyce singled out Édouard Dujardin as the originator of the internal monologue, the French novelist—after the fact—delivered the lecture in which he attempted to define what he had discovered half a century before. This was published with the portentous title: *Le monologue intérieur, son apparition, ses origines, sa place dans l'œuvre de James Joyce et dans le roman contemporain.* It is something less than the treatise the title suggests; and Dujardin actually speaks of it as an "attempt" at a definition. His general conclusions are:

The internal monologue, like every monologue, is the speech of a given character, designed to introduce us directly into the internal life of this character, without the author's intervening by explaining or commenting, and like every monologue, is a discourse without listener and a discourse unspoken;

but it differs from the traditional monologue in that:

as regards its substance, it expresses the most intimate thoughts, those closest to the unconscious;

as regards its spirit, it is discourse before any logical organization, reproducing thought in its original state and as it comes into the mind;

as for its form, it is expressed by means of direct sentences reduced to a syntactic minimum;

thus it responds essentially to the conception which we have today of poetry.

From this analysis, serving as preamble, he derives the following more concise definition:

The internal monologue, in its nature of the order of poetry, is that unheard and unspoken speech by which a character expresses his inmost thoughts, those lying nearest the unconscious, without regard to logical organization—that is, in their original state—by means of direct sentences reduced to syntactic minimum, and in such a way as to give the impression of reproducing the thoughts just as they come into the mind.

The preamble and definition mix things up somewhat. It is confusing to have the word "speech" or "discourse" introduced in alluding to something "unheard and unspoken." Use of the words implies also that we think always on the verbal level, whereas the "thoughts just as they come into the mind," as Dujardin himself recognized, sensory, image-laden and fragmented, are often beyond words. Above all, the concept that "internal monologue" expresses those thoughts "closest to the unconscious" suggests a misunderstanding of the nature of the unconscious. Stephen Spender makes exactly the same mistake in *The Destructive Element* when he labels the chapter devoted to Joyce and James "The Unconscious."

The present inquiry is concerned exclusively with consciousness as rendered in fiction; but it is necessary to make clear the distinction between consciousness and the unconscious which can never be rendered but only deduced.

There are few things more difficult to explain than the unconscious. Many persons, indeed, deny its existence,

54

even though there has been an awareness of it, in greater or lesser degree, from early times. It was not invented by Freud, as some would have us believe. The teachings of modern psycho-analysis have shown (and we have daily evidence of it in our own lives if we know how to observe it) that an unconscious level of experience is constituted within us whose *conscious* patterns may be read only by those especially qualified to do so. We ourselves are vouchsafed only occasional glimpses into it. It can be read only in terms of those thoughts and fantasies which we bring *into consciousness*. I think I can offer an illustration. There exists an unpublished letter at Harvard University written by Henry James in 1884. In it he promises a serial to the editor of the *Atlantic Monthly* for the year 1885. However, three times in this letter, so clearly of 1884, Henry James makes the same slip of the pen: he writes 1865 instead of 1885 as the year for which he promises the serial. Had it happened once, we might lay it to inadvertence; but thrice, and then uncorrected, means that James's *unconscious* substituted 1865 for 1885, and he remained unaware of what he had done. I exclude the possibility of conscious intention, since there was no palpable reason for giving a wrong year in a serious business letter. *The slip of the pen, therefore, was a clear signature of his unconscious.* We can formulate as many theories as we like about the reasons for this slip of the pen; but all we can say definitely is that some part of James's unconscious led his hand to write a wrong year not once but thrice—a year two decades removed from the year he wanted to write. The record itself is no longer unconscious, since we can see it and recognize it; the "1865" is the symbol by which we recognize some element in the Jamesian unconscious.

In a word, the unconscious cannot be expressed in its own unconscious form, since obviously this is unconscious. *We can only infer it from symbols emerging in the conscious expressions of the person*, such as remembered dreams, fantasies, or slips of the tongue or of the pen. Thus when Édouard Dujardin speaks of the area "closest to the unconscious," what he is really referring to is that peripheral area, outside the central stream of thought, to which we do not always attend, but which is the "halo" or "fringe" of impression described by William James. The use of the word "unconscious" by Dujardin can only create confusion. It takes us to areas which are beyond rendering save in some substitutive, symbolic *but still conscious* form.

2

The term "internal monologue" was used at first interchangeably with the term "stream of consciousness." Harry Levin, in his critical study of Joyce, expressed a preference for it, stating that "the internal monologue lends itself more readily to critical analysis than the more illusory stream of consciousness." Neither term covers all cases; one or the other can be used as a critical convenience; but it must be recognized that the word "monologue," because of its association with the theatre, has distinct literary and dramatic connotations that do not convey the idea of flux. In the traditional monologue—in its original Greek sense it was a "speaking alone"—the character gives the audience logical and reasoned thoughts. These are selective even while they represent casual reflection or reverie, and are rendered without relation to external stimuli. Hamlet's "To be or not to be," read by itself, out of the context of the play, gives us no feeling of his surroundings or the sensory experiences he may be having at the time of utterance. His monologue, or soliloquy, reflects and expresses his inner tension, the conflicts of his troubled spirit: his measured thoughts have been distilled from the fluid stream of consciousness to which, in this case, we have no access, since all the impurities have been filtered out. If, by making a pastiche of Shakespeare and Joyce, we were to insert some of the impurities, the result would certainly be what neither Shakespeare nor Joyce would have intended, but it serves to illustrate our point:

> To be or not to be that is the question
> The ghost—th' agenbite of inwit; he pandied me!
> What is this stench? the slings, the arrows, ah! cruel

56

Outrageous fortune. Clang! Who tolls the bell?
Modality ineluctable. To sleep
Perchance to dream; aye there's the rub.

Here Hamlet is no longer lost in thought: ideas come to
him by association: the memory of his father's ghost reminds him of the bite of inner guilt; some recollection of
a boyish punishment, perhaps related to the feeling of
guilt. Then an unpleasant odour is noticed, but his mind
jumps from this to the slings and arrows—the cruel ups
and downs—of one's fortunes, and a clanging bell im-
pinges upon this thought. From the bell his mind leaps to
the ineluctable modality of the visible, and the blessing of
sleep which erases the visible and substitutes dreams. In
a word, our pastiche is monologue to which has been
added the direct verbal expression of associations and
sensory perceptions. The words "internal monologue"
inadequately describe the fluid and unorganized state of
thought we have tried to suggest as existing in Hamlet's
mind. The descriptive words "stream of consciousness"
seem more apposite.

Eugene O'Neill, in *Strange Interlude*, probably under the
influence of the writings of Joyce, made a direct attempt
to introduce stream of consciousness on the stage. As
produced by the Theatre Guild, the play consisted of the
usual speeches of the characters, who also, however, spoke
their thoughts using a different vocal inflection. All action
on stage was momentarily arrested and frozen, while the
thoughts were uttered. In doing this, however, O'Neill
was employing merely the time-honoured "asides" of the
old plays or a series of soliloquies. Thus at the beginning
of the play Marsden enters. His spoken speech is "I'll
wait in here, Mary," and then we are ushered into his
thoughts:

How perfectly the Professor's unique haven! . . . Primly
classical . . . when New Englander meets Greek! . . . He hasn't
added one book in years . . . how old was I when I first came
here? . . . six . . . with my father . . . father . . . how dim his
face has grown! . . . he wanted to speak to me just before he
died . . . the hospital . . . smell of iodoform in the cool halls
. . . hot summer . . . I bent down . . . his voice had withdrawn

far away . . . I couldn't understand him . . . what son can ever understand? . . . always too near, too soon, too distant or too late.

The thought associations in this passage are rendered in a fairly logical progression; what we are given essentially is a chain of memory without intrusion of external stimuli and no representation of peripheral thought. This can be called "internal monologue." Nevertheless, we must recognize that whatever critical terms we may apply to O'Neill's experiment, he seems to have created the illusion for the play's audiences that they were participating in the mental life of the characters.

We must not lose ourselves in a search for label-definitions; nor should we attempt to make them tightly fit certain works that can better be described than labelled. The term "internal monologue" becomes merely a useful designation for certain works of fiction of sustained subjectivity, written from a single point of view, in which the writer himself narrows down the stream of consciousness and places us largely at the "centre" of the character's thoughts—that centre where thought often uses words rather than images. To understand the problems involved alike for writer and reader we can turn to Dujardin's pioneer experiment. It has many things to teach us about the psychological novel of our time.

CHAPTER V

A SYMBOLIST EXPERIMENT

THE EXTENT to which Édouard Dujardin erected his definition of "internal monologue" *post factum* becomes clear when we read *Les lauriers sont coupés*, which in translation by Stuart Gilbert was called *We'll to the Woods No More*. One gains the impression from it that Dujardin arrived at his definition as much from a reading of Joyce as from a re-reading of himself. In dismissing his novel as slight and unimportant, criticism has overlooked the singular historical interest of the work and the illumination it casts upon a writer's struggle to render flowing thought. James Joyce, in advising Valéry Larbaud to read the book, told him that he would find himself, "from the very first line, posted within the mind of the protagonist." Larbaud quoted Joyce as saying: "It is the continuous unfolding of his thoughts which, replacing normal objective narration, depicts to us his acts and experiences."

The entire book is quotation from the mind of its hero. Dujardin recognized that to create an illusion of mental flux he would have to give an effect of thoughts entering his hero's mind at random. On the other hand, he struggled constantly with the problem of setting his scenes and carrying on the action. Let us walk with Dujardin's hero into a restaurant (as we will later do with Joyce's Leopold Bloom). We do not yet know his name. That will be revealed to us progressively in the later pages of the book. We know that on this soft, warm April evening in Paris he has a rendezvous with an actress. We know that the year is 1887, since in the opening pages, the hero was told by a friend that he intended to see *Ruy Blas* that very evening at the Théâtre-Français and the thought that entered the hero's mind was: "The idea of going to see *Ruy Blas* in 1887!" We know it is a warm, soft April evening because, rather opportunely, that was in the hero's thought in the opening paragraphs of the book.

Red and gold [he has entered the restaurant], a glare of light, the café; flashing mirrors; a white-aproned waiter; pillars hung with hats and overcoats. Anyone here I know? Those people are watching me come in; a thin chap with long whiskers, looks the regular heavy father. All the tables taken, where shall I sit? An empty place down there, capital, my usual table; why shouldn't a fellow have his favourite table? Nothing for Leah to laugh at in that.

—Yes, sir?

The waiter. The table. My hat on the peg. Take gloves off; drop them casually on the table, beside the plate; or shall I in my overcoat pocket? No, on the table; it's trifles like that show a fellow's style. Hang up my coat now; sit down; that's better; really fagged I was. Yes, I'll put my gloves in the overcoat pocket after all.

The scene has its parallel—much more intricately written—in *Ulysses*. The internal monologue here can only be described as "primitive," and yet it conveys a sufficient degree of reality. It is not altogether convincing to have us believe that the preoccupied man would necessarily bring into the centre of his consciousness the table, the hat on the peg, the removal of his gloves; these would be registered almost automatically by anyone who has removed his gloves many times before or placed his hat on many pegs in many restaurants. This said, it must be acknowledged that such thoughts are conceivable in a person self-consciously concerned about the figure he is cutting in the presence of the other diners. In terms of fictional verisimilitude the thoughts—waiter, table, hat on peg, gloves—seem to be serving as the equivalent of stage directions in a play, and the hero figures as an actor, whose every move has been calculated. But the reality would be a simultaneous registering of the items tabulated by Dujardin in the hero's mind, and doubtless beyond the verbal level.

Dujardin incorporates into the monologue not only these "stage directions," but his scenic descriptions. At the opening of the book:

The hour is striking six, the hour I waited for. Here is the house I have to enter, where I shall meet someone; the house; the hall; let's go in.

Once he is inside:

The stairs; the first steps. Supposing he has left early; he sometimes does; but I have got to tell him the story of my day. The first landing; wide, bright staircase; windows.

The only non-descriptive thought, indeed the only genuine reflection in this passage that has some logic on the verbal level is "Supposing he has left early."

We can readily observe Dujardin manœuvring to remain inside his hero's mind while seeking to impart to the reader the data customarily given by the omniscient author in conventional fiction. Midway through the book the effort breaks down. The reader is not yet in possession of the complete story of the hero's romance with the actress. Feeling still the need to impart every last detail, Dujardin grafts on to his text a reading by Daniel Prince (it is in this portion that we discover his name) of all the letters he has received from the object of his affection. From his correspondence we learn the extent of his vanity and the way in which he is the dupe of the actress. We learn also of the fascination she exercises upon him.

The narrative awkwardnesses must not be allowed to distract us from the positive elements in the work. If we begin with a sense of impatience and a feeling that Dujardin has willy-nilly made a grab-bag of image and phrase in Prince's mind, we find ourselves by degrees gathered into the story, pulled along in it by a certain charm as well as by the suspense aroused by Dujardin—the suspense of whether on this night Daniel Prince will succeed in his amatory quest. We have a very real, and even acute, sense of being in the Paris of 1887; we feel the softness of the evening on the boulevards, we saunter with the hero in his top-hat and his gloves, we are aware of his self-consciousness, we gape with him at the girls, we light the candle in his dressing-room, and almost feel the fresh cold water he splashes on his face. And finally, standing with

61

him on his balcony, we are caught up in the atmosphere of his mind and in his reverie:

I lean on the balcony, bending over the emptiness of space; I take deep breaths of the evening air, vaguely conscious of that loveliness outside, the shadowed, soft, forlorn remoteness of the air, all this night's beauty; a grey-black sky, here and there suffused with blue, and tiny stars, like tremulous drops of water, watery stars; all around, the misty paleness of open sky; over yonder a solid gloom of trees and beyond, black houses with lighted windows; roofs, dingy roofs; below, blurred together, the garden; a chaos of tangled walls and all sorts of things; black houses with lighted windows; and, above me, the sky, vast, bluish, whitened with its early stars; mild air, no wind, air warm with the breath of early May. There is warmth, a soft caress, in this velvety night air; the trees down there are a patch of gloom beneath the grey-blue circle of sky, spangled with tremulous gleams; and vague shadows brood in the garden of night.

This may seem more like description of a series of images than of thought. The passage, however, is evocative, and it assumes reality for us because we are by now firmly inside the mind of Daniel Prince. We are looking with Prince from his balcony: what he mirrors for us, we see. Gradually the form of the actress (in Daniel's mind—and ours) merges with the night:

I see your beauty and your grace; divinely graceful as you move, the even cadence of your limbs; and languid your steps on the carpet beside the table with the flowers, in your delicious yellow room, yes, languidly you walk across a sheen of flowered softness, slowly leaning now this way, now that, palely smiling, your ivory face framed in frolic gold, smiling, slowly swaying as you pass, you pass before me; your light gown of creamy muslin floats about you, rippling where a ribbon flutters, gathered muslin moulding your bosom, your limbs, the young grace of your body; and softly your lips are moving; lovedear, I love you so. Tall shadows of trees climb skywards, high on high; and mine, all mine, you glimmer in the pale shadows, smiling, simple sweet and kind.

What is clear from these passages is that Dujardin, the symbolist and friend of Mallarmé, although writing a novel that is a projection of symbolist theory—the rendering of the evanescence of experience—actually tries to set down in concrete terms the sense perceptions of his hero which generally are not expressed on a verbal level. With few exceptions the words he uses are not highly imaged or nuanced, but direct and concrete. If the book is not rich in the metaphors we have come to regard as an integral part of symbolist expression, it does seem to be indulging in what might best be described as a kind of *impressionism*. As Daniel leans over the balcony, the scene he looks at, reflected in his mind, can remind one of an impressionist painting. Perhaps the only symbolist touch one finds in the passage itself is Daniel's image of the stars as "tremulous drops of water."

One passage comes closer to what we might call stream-of-consciousness writing than the recording of internal monologue. In the warmth of the actress's room, and with her head on his shoulder, the young hero floats away into a daydream that carries him to the verge of sleep. It makes us wonder whether he does not prefer his dream of the actress to the reality of making love to her:

This is her body; the rise and fall of her breast, her blended fragrance, oh lovely April night! . . . Presently we shall be driving together . . . in cool air . . . we will go out . . . quite soon . . . the two candles . . . along the boulevards . . . *I love my turkeys and my sheep, But oh I love you more* . . . That street girl with the bold eyes and cherry lips . . . the room, high fireplace . . . the dining room . . . my father . . . sitting together, we three, father, mother, I . . . why is mother so pale? . . . she is watching me . . . we shall dine, yes, in the garden . . . the servant . . . bring the table . . . Leah . . . she is laying the table . . . my father . . . the concierge . . . with a letter . . . a letter from her? . . . thanks . . . a ripple, a murmur, skies uprising, high on high.

In this novel we discover again that we must read on two levels of awareness: we can, if we achieve identification with Daniel Prince, ride with him in the carriage beside the beautiful woman; but we are also appraising him—standing off from him, evaluating his own testimony, and seeing him from the outside for the dupe that he is. He emerges as a character both *felt* and seen: we watch his self-intoxication and note his vanity and his

63

illusions; we also sense the Paris around him, all early spring and soft, and are aware of a time removed from our own. As we turn back over the pages of the book we discover we have lived the story in spite of its absurdities: the novel has conveyed an atmosphere, created a character, given us an almost uncanny time-sense, teased our mind with a gentle curiosity: will Daniel Prince succeed in his amatory quest on this night in 1887, or will the actress rebuff him anew?

Any account of such a novel represents a pulling-together of disparate elements of the story. It is in *my* mind that the disorderly thoughts, presented out of sequence, have been reshuffled into some semblance of order. In reading this novel, in listening to Daniel Prince's internal monologue with a third ear, I have rewritten the novel. The question that now must be asked is this: Would all readers read such novels in a similar manner?

CHAPTER VI

THE READER'S VISION

WOULD ALL readers read such novels in a similar manner? The question is at the very heart of our inquiry.

There are, in Proust, certain admirable pages on the reading of fiction. In real life, he observes, people are too opaque, they represent too much physical mass, too much of a "dead weight which our sensibilities have not the strength to lift." People in books, however, are more readily assimilated. Since our experience of people, in life or in books, is through our mind and our feelings, the fictitious persons can take on a reality more intense than the real persons, for "we have made them our own, since it is in ourselves that they are happening." And Proust goes on to say:

Once the novelist has brought us to that state, in which, as in all purely mental states, every emotion is multiplied ten-fold, into which his book comes to disturb us as might a dream, but a dream more lucid, and of a more lasting impression, than those which come to us in sleep; why, then, for the space of an hour he sets free within us all the joys and sorrows in the world, a few of which, only, we should have to spend years of our actual life in getting to know, and the keenest, the most intense of which would never have been revealed to us because the slow course of their development stops our perception of them.

Thus Proust discovered, as Henry James had done before him, that the writer of fiction can not only represent life but can actually create it for a reader—a reader sufficiently attentive and responsive to what he is reading.

An important distinction must be drawn between the material most readers can grasp in a novel and that part of it which becomes, in effect, a part of our personal mental dream-state. We all read the same words on the printed page and gather from them a similar meaning;

our intellect grasps the essential content and the data furnished by the novelist; we can discuss the book with another reader in perfect agreement as to the kind of story it has to tell. But the question recurs: do we *experience* the book in the same way? How many persons have felt terror upon reading a ghostly tale such as *The Turn of the Screw*, only to discover, in surprise, that a fellow reader "couldn't get through the book"? How many readers have shed real tears over some trivial romantic book they knew to be unreal, while other readers shrugged their shoulders and laughed? Between the book *read* and the book *felt* there lie all the differences of opinion that divide reader and reader, critic and critic. Rare are the readers who can achieve a balance between intellectual apprehension of a novel and an intense feeling of it. Yet it is for the feeling as much as the intellectual apprehension that most novelists write their work.

This is particularly true of the modern psychological novel. Here the entire work, by its very nature, offers us the data in higgledy-piggledy disorder. We are asked to *see into* the characters, to make deductions from such data as may be offered us—and at the same time to *live* for ourselves the experience with which we are confronted on the printed page. This is asking a great deal of the reader, and it explains why encounters between writers and readers (on the printed page) are so varied and so contradictory. The critical reader who intellectually apprehends a book but has achieved no particular feeling in the process usually has only a ledger-book concept of the work. He can retell the story, give the ages of the characters or describe what they look like, discourse upon the logic of the tale told, yet his discourse will be comparatively lifeless—though it may be as exact as figures in a ledger or statistics in a document. At the other extreme is the reader who has *felt* every page of the work, but can give us no coherent account of the data and is happy even to be able to give a reasonable account (difficult enough at any time) of the experience of the reading.

Let us look at Dorothy Richardson's *Pointed Roofs*, the first volume or "chapter" of her twelve-volume *Pilgrimage*.* About the entire work there are extremes of opinion —some readers find it unreadable and "impossible" while others speak of it with high emotion. Whether we are able to read it or not we must accept its "pioneer" place in the history of the twentieth-century novel. Miss Richardson set herself a difficult experiment, perhaps more difficult in a technical sense than Proust's: like her French contemporary she placed the reader in the mind of a single character, and with great tenacity of purpose held to her difficult task until it was completed. The twelve "chapters" deal exclusively with the pilgrimage of Miriam Henderson's mind from adolescence to middle life.

At this point in the inquiry it seems to me that I can best discuss the entire question of the reader's relation to the novel of subjectivity by drawing upon my own experience in the reading of *Pointed Roofs*. I read it first two decades ago and found I could develop no interest in Miriam Henderson and her emotional adventures in the German boarding-school to which she goes to teach the English language. The volume indeed discouraged me from reading any of its successors, and it seemed to me that the great defect of the book was that Dorothy Richardson had selected too dull a mind for her experiment.

Returning to *Pointed Roofs* after two decades, I found once more that my interest lagged. The author was involving me in a world of chirping females, and I had to force myself to absorb the contents of each page. The heroine struck me as immature and wholly without interest. I had begun by imagining her in the first pages as a rather prim Victorian type, perhaps twenty-five, who had just packed her new Saratoga trunk and was being

* The volumes are titled: *Pointed Roofs, Backwater, Honeycomb, The Tunnel, Interim, Deadlock, Revolving Lights, The Trap, Oberland, Dawn's Left Hand, Clear Horizon, Dimple Hill.*

escorted with Victorian decorum to her first job, on the Continent, in a German school at Hanover. The sense of her being an older person despite her youthful behaviour seemed confirmed when after about fifty pages "Miriam sat up stiffly—adjusted her pince-nez—and desperately ordered the reading to begin again." It was, however, difficult to relate this Miriam of the pince-nez to the Miriam constantly being revealed in the book, a creature of variable moods, now measured and grave, now mercurial.

I had read some fifty pages when I suddenly encountered this startling (to me) sentence: "She knew her pince-nez disguised her . . . , and she was only seventeen and a half." Miriam, wearing her Victorian pince-nez is not yet eighteen! (She turns eighteen and puts up her hair for the first time in the opening pages of the second volume, *Backwater*.) Thus my whole judgment of the first volume had been coloured by an erroneous impression produced by the pince-nez, the Saratoga trunk, the "grown-up" airs assumed by Miriam and my failure to note earlier clues to her exact age.

In a conventional novel I would have known Miriam Henderson's age from the start. I would have understood clearly those moods of late adolescence, the chirping scenes of the opening pages which had reminded me of the novels of Louisa May Alcott, the general ecstatic quality of some of the passages of her internal monologue. But the picture was blurred; I was reading the novel with an unfocused vision. What was more, even after it was clear to me that Miriam was not yet eighteen, the full effect of this revelation did not sink in promptly. It was a gradual process, requiring a slow focusing of my own mental pince-nez. Looking back across the pages to rediscover my experience as a reader, I found the scene, the important scene, in which the book quite suddenly changed in my hands from a lifeless dead weight of paper and print, to a living thing, from a work I was intellectually absorbing, and finding tedious, to a work charged with feeling and life. It occurred when I began to re-read certain sections of the book in the light of my newly-acquired picture of Miriam.

The particular scene that performed the curious change in my relationship to the book occurs when Miriam, in·a mood of elation, is singing to herself that she will be going to visit "Pom-pom-pom-er-ania" and bursts into the school hall there to discover the Swiss Pastor Lahmann near the window. "You are vairy happy, mademoiselle," he says to her. She responds in a way to which we have become accustomed: she likes men, but they also frighten her. She likes the pastor's "comforting black mannishness" and at the same time is so put off by him that she blandly denies she is in a happy mood. The pastor quietly talks to her and remarks among other things that he has a fondness for the English verse,

> "A little land, well-tilled,
> A little wife, well-willed,
> And great riches."

Miriam seemed to gaze long at a pallid, rounded man with smiling eyes. She saw a garden and fields, a firelit interior, a little woman smiling and busy and agreeable moving quickly about . . . and Pastor Lahmann—presiding. It filled her with fury to be regarded as one of a world of little tame things to be summoned by little men to be well-willed wives. She must make him see that she did not even recognize such a thing as "a well-willed wife." She felt her gaze growing fixed and moved to withdraw it and herself.

But the pastor quite suddenly changes the subject.

"Why do you wear glasses, mademoiselle?"
The voice was full of sympathetic wistfulness.
"I have a severe myopic astigmatism," she announced, gathering up her music and feeling the words as little hammers on the newly seen, pallid, rounded face.
"Dear me . . . I wonder whether the glasses are really necessary. . . . May I look at them? . . . I know something of eyework."
Miriam detached her tightly fitting pince-nez and, having given them up, stood with her music in hand anxiously watching. Half her vision gone with her glasses, she saw only a dim black-coated knowledge, near at hand, going perhaps to help her.
"You wear them always—for how long?"

69

"Poor child, poor child, and you must have passed through all your schooling with those lame, lame eyes . . . let me see the eyes . . . turn a little to the light . . . so."

Standing near and large he scrutinized her vague gaze.

"And sensitive to light, too. You were vairy, vairy blonde, even more blonde than you are now, as a child, mademoiselle?"

"Na guten tag, Herr Pastor."

Fräulein Pfaff's smiling voice sounded from the little door.

Pastor Lahmann stepped back.

Now the book was alive for me, not only because there had been a moment of drama, an encounter between an adolescent English girl and a benign and paternal Swiss pastor, but because in some way some quality of feeling had disengaged itself from the pages—or been disengaged within me. What had performed this extraordinary change, so that now I could see Miriam, see the schoolroom, hear the pastor's accent, feel sorry for her nearsightedness and her uneasiness with men? I turned to other passages. Everywhere now Miriam was real, palpable; formerly dull pages warmed into new interest and new life. I went back and started the book from the beginning. Now I was able to read it through with no sense of tedium. Delicate shades of feeling were there, and moments of the heroine's experience—sunsets, a storm, the very sense of Hanover's streets, the rigidities of Fräulein Pfaff, the music in the evenings, the tremulous awarenesses of the young girls in the school—all this which had seemed inconsequential before now had validity, even though the book had no story and nothing happened that was not part of the ordinary events in a girls' school, such as the girls washing their hair, or talking about their boy friends.

What had happened? It was important to understand. And as I searched the memory of my own reading it seemed to me that I had somehow begun by struggling against Dorothy Richardson: she had wanted me to enter into the mind of a young adolescent—a female adolescent—and I had not been able to do this. I could not adopt the one "point of view" she offered me, an angle of vision that required more identification than I—

as indeed many of her male readers—could achieve. It is doubtless much easier for a man to enter into the mind of Daniel Prince going to a rendezvous with an actress than the mind of a moody young English girl in a German girls' school. The episode with Pastor Lahmann, however, had offered me the key. And as I studied it closely I saw that what had happened here was that *through* Miriam Henderson's angle of vision of the pastor I had finally entered the book. She had made me aware of him, and it was with him I could identify myself. So that while we see him only as Miriam sees him, it became suddenly possible for me, the male reader, to feel myself standing in front of this blonde English girl and inquiring into her near-sightedness. The alchemy of this was that—as Proust observed, "since it is in ourselves that they are happening"—Miriam now became real for me and remained real. At last I could experience her as Dorothy Richardson doubtless wanted me to: a near-sighted English girl translated between a certain March and July from Victorian London to a German school, experiencing the strangeness of the German world, swinging between euphoria and depression, reaching out with the heightened sensitivity of adolescence to her environment, experiencing assaults of feeling in her relationships with the girls in the school, uncertain of her feelings about men. The general effect of the book—and the feelings I had contributed to my re-reading of it—seemed to have brought me close to the reality Dorothy Richardson had sought to create.

2

This was my experience as a persistent and searching reader. It was not at all clear that any generalization could be made from this experience. I did, however, feel that it might be fruitful to ask for the testimony of other readers. I had noted the extent to which some of the male members of my Princeton seminar had actually resented being manœuvred by Dorothy Richardson into the mind of an adolescent girl. On the other hand, a woman student in my seminar at New York University spoke of

71

Miriam's mind as "a delicate instrument" and described the excitement experienced in observing the heroine through the "peep-holes of her mind." A distinguished English novelist, a woman, told me that reading Dorothy Richardson had been one of the richest experiences of her youth. An American poet, a woman, described to me how she had read the book not as a whole, but by discovering Miriam's emotions and her sensual and perceptual experiences from page to page. And on seeing Miss Richardson's volumes in the home of another woman, she also a poet, I pursued my inquiry by asking what her reading of these books had yielded her. The incisive reply was "intensities."

Perhaps the only generalization possible, then, is that, in a novel which uses internal monologue as Dorothy Richardson did, the author succeeds only when the reader achieves a certain state of identification or relationship with the sole mind that is offered to him in the pages of the book. But I suspect also that for the many the problem lies in the need to see a wholeness that can be achieved only after all the disparate facts have been gathered. This is what Joseph Frank meant when he observed that a stream-of-consciousness novel cannot be "read" in the usual sense—it can only be re-read. In re-reading we have the heightened awareness that has come to us from what was at first not so much a reading of the book as an exploration of its content. This, however, must be slightly amended to include the experience of the two women poets who, in the real sense, *read* the book, without the need for re-reading. For them, I suppose, there was no need to grasp the continuum of Miriam's experience—since the poet may focus his attention on a flower, a tree, a bird, a cloud, discovering beauty in each and making of each a wholeness complete in itself. Or, to return to the stream image, they can float on the stream of consciousness seeing only what is in the stream at a given moment without the need to look behind to see what has gone before or to know the direction that is being taken.

3

Dorothy Richardson offered no theories about her work. The experiment itself sufficed. In an interview she once expressed her dissatisfaction with the phrase "stream of consciousness," asserting that "amongst the company of useful labels devised to meet the exigencies of literary criticism it stands alone, isolated by its perfect imbecility." And she went on to give her concept of the flux of experience, which amounted to a description of what she had tried to convey in her rendering of Miriam Henderson's mind:

The "mind" may be, or may become, anything from a rag-bag to a madhouse. It may wobble continuously or may be more or less steadily focused. But its central core, luminous point (call it what you will, its names are legion), though more or less continuously expanding from birth to maturity, remains stable, one with itself throughout life.

Her novel is, indeed, built round a series of "luminous points"—what the poet described as "intensities"—and Miriam Henderson remains most of the time the "central core." A heightened awareness of Miriam should not blind us to the limitations of Dorothy Richardson's creation. We can sometimes feel ourselves to be trapped spectators in the mind of a woman possessing no marked personality, often sentimental and belligerently feminine and rather unimaginative, yet having extraordinary flashes of insight which redeem many turgid pages. Miss Richardson's literary style improved in the later volumes, but great plateaux of aridity surround the "intensities." However, she opened a new pathway, cleared the ground, exerted an unmistakable influence.

When she gathered together the twelve parts of *Pilgrimage* into a four-volume collected edition in 1938 she wrote a rather elliptical Foreword to the series. In it she described how the choice for her, in 1911, when she started writing, was between realists like Balzac and her contemporary Arnold Bennett, or men who were writing novels of satire and protest. She determined to produce "a feminine equivalent of the current masculine realism,"

73

but became aware, as she wrote, of "a stranger in the form of contemplated reality having for the first time . . . its own way." This "contemplated reality" revealed a hundred faces "any of which, the moment it was entrapped within the close mesh of direct statement, summoned its fellows to disquality it." She acknowledged that Henry James might have taught her how to keep "the reader incessantly watching the conflict of human forces through the eye of a single observer." However, she suggested that Goethe had long ago defined the subjective novel:

In the novel [wrote Goethe] reflections and incidents should be featured; in drama character and action. The novel must proceed slowly and the thought processes of the principal figure must, by one device or another, hold up the development of the whole.

What Dorothy Richardson stated in her Foreword, which was probably her final word on the subject, is to be found in another form in *Dawn's Left Hand,* the tenth "chapter" of *Pilgrimage.* She speaks here of the "self-satisfied, complacent, know-all condescendingness" which she contends James and Conrad displayed in their handling of their materials. Wells seemed to her "to have more awareness," but, she observes, "all his books are witty exploitations of ideas." And she adds: "The torment of *all* novels is what is left out. . . . Bang, bang, bang, on they go, these men's books, like an L.C.C. tram, yet unable to make you forget them, the authors, for a moment."

What novels left out, if we are to judge by what Dorothy Richardson put in, are whole areas of feeling, self-preoccupation and reverie, combined with sensory experience. The swings in mood of the heroine serve only to intensify our awareness of reality; out of this alternation of the evanescent and the concrete, Miriam ultimately emerges a rounded, one might say a three-dimensional, figure—just so long as we can stay with her and bear up under certain inevitable *longueurs*—stay with her and *feel* with her as we follow the play of her mind.

CHAPTER VII

THE MIND'S EYE VIEW

PUBLICATION OF *Ulysses* in 1922 was a thunderclap in the world of letters more resounding in its time than the thunderclap of *Madame Bovary* three-quarters of a century before. Like Gustave Flaubert, James Joyce had produced a calculated work of art to which he had dedicated himself for years, with a versatility of craftsmanship far surpassing this one among his several masters. Like its predecessor, *Ulysses* was intended to astonish the world—and there is little doubt of the effect it has had upon a whole generation of writers. If Flaubert wrote into his novel his inner rage against the bourgeoisie, Joyce's work was an act of vengeance against an Ireland which (as Joyce insisted in one of his broadsides) sent its writers into banishment. In truth Joyce-Dedalus, the writer who had soared on literary wings over Europe, had banished himself, and using his own selected tools—silence, exile, cunning—had forged a complex labyrinth: forged it by the light of aesthetic theories hammered out in the days of his youth. It was Joyce who, possessing an incomparable mastery of words, succeeded above all writers in capturing the atmosphere of the mind. The cunning artificer who could construct a labyrinth could also dare the labyrinth of consciousness. With him the inward turning penetrated to the deepest recesses of mental experience. He is the fountain-head of the modern psychological novel.

I

Édouard Dujardin, in his stumbling awkward way, begins *Les lauriers sont coupés* by pin-pointing the moment in the year of his novel.

So time and place come to a point: it is the Now and Here [*c'est l'aujourd'hui, c'est l'ici*] this hour that is striking, all around me life; the time and place, an April evening, Paris.

In *Ulysses*, Stephen Dedalus, mentally preparing himself for his discussion of Shakespeare in the library scene, thinks:

Hold to the now, the here, through which all future plunges to the past.

And this recalls Bergson's "the invisible progress of the past, which gnaws into the future." Dedalus, however, has inverted the thought, and by doing so accented the present.

That moment, the Here, which becomes the past even as it is uttered or felt, is what Joyce addressed himself to catch in *Ulysses*. The modern epic, as conceived by Joyce, was originally to have been a short story in *Dubliners*. Although extended to a length far beyond anything in that volume of brief tales, it is still conceived as a moment in all time. Joyce re-created the life of an entire city in a fixed period, some eighteen hours, the date 16 June, 1904, from morning to the early hours of the next morning. He was at the same time placing this day in the history of all time, so that it becomes eighteen hours set in all the centuries, indeed in that eternity which is evoked so remarkably in one of the sermons in *A Portrait of the Artist as a Young Man*: he would create a microcosm in the cosmos, he would pick up that grain of sand which in all eternity would not even be the merest of mere fragments of the mountain. Let us listen with Dedalus to the words of the sermon in the *Portrait*:

You have often seen the sand on the seashore. How fine are its tiny grains! And how many of those tiny little grains go to make up the small handful which a child grasps in its play. Now imagine a mountain of that sand, a million miles high, reaching from the earth to the farthest heavens, and a million miles broad, extending to remotest space, and a million miles in thickness; and imagine such an enormous mass of countless particles of sand multiplied as often as there are leaves in the forest, drops of water in the mighty ocean, feathers on birds, scales on fish, hairs on animals, atoms in the vast expanse of the air: and imagine that at the end of every million years a little bird came to that mountain and carried away in its beak a tiny grain of that sand. How many millions upon millions of centuries would pass before that bird had carried away even a square foot of that mountain, how many eons upon eons of ages before it had carried away all? Yet at the end of that immense stretch of time not even one instant of eternity could be said to have ended. At the end of all those billions and trillions of years eternity would have scarcely begun.

Is it any wonder that Joyce, the young artist, caught in that nightmare of time, time without end, sought to wrest a single day from it and to enclose it hard and fast in the integument of words?

This was the great frame, his subject in all its arrogant grandeur. His experiment transcended by far the first stages of the novel of subjectivity. Proust and Dorothy Richardson had confined themselves to a single consciousness. Joyce, at one leap, went beyond them to capture the atmosphere of the mind. He not only carried his principal character forward from one volume to the next, as they had done, but he began to spin two other consciousnesses parallel to that of the young Stephen Dedalus. In addition, he would give us brief glimpses into the minds of a host of other Dublin characters: Father Conmee of Clongowes who had befriended Dedalus years before; Miss Dunne, the typist, who is carrying on a correspondence with Bloom although they have never met; Master Patrick Aloysius Dignam, whose father had been buried that morning. We hear many people in this book and catch the flow of their minds; nearly always, however, we do so through other eyes—and largely through the mind's eye view of Stephen Dedalus or Leopold Bloom.

In the multiple-scene chapter in which Joyce presents the panorama of Dublin and fills it with multiple incidents, people, minds, we become the collective eye of all the characters: for Joyce, using a technical device since much imitated, sews these scenes together with the thread of the vice-regal cavalcade that drives through the streets, ringing steel, while all the characters turn to look at the carriage. We are in Dublin—in all of it—and then always back again in the minds of Dedalus and Bloom, where we see its reflection. There is much more to this strange work than the stream of consciousness of the characters: there

77

is the Homeric frame, the literary parodies, the actual newspaper events of 16 June (that day that was to be forever after "Bloomsday" in Joyce's personal calendar). The day begins with a funeral and ends with a birth. The past disappears into the present, the future disappears into the present; both present and future become the past. And Dedalus, in the library, displaying his wit and his pedantry, explains how the artist weaves and unweaves his image in time. Past and present may be in an external flux; but it is possible to find a continuing point of reference:

As the mole on my right breast is where it was when I was born, though all my body has been woven of new stuff time after time, so through the ghost of the unquiet father the image of the unliving son looks forth. In the intense instant of imagination, when the mind, Shelley says, is a fading coal that which I was is that which I am and that which in possibility I may come to be. So in the future, the sister of the past, I may see myself as I sit here now but by reflection from that which then I shall be.

2

We meet Stephen Dedalus on the first page of *Ulysses*. When we enter his mind for the first time on the third page it is to discover, in full force, the leitmotiv of his consciousness, during this particular day in Dublin. Step by step, Buck Mulligan has brought us round to it; he looks at the sea and calls it "a grey sweet mother," "our great sweet mother," and then "our mighty mother." The theme has been struck, *fortissimo*. Mulligan turns his "great searching eyes" from the sea to Stephen's face and upbraids him for his failure to kneel and pray by the bedside of his dying mother. And now Stephen's thoughts announce what will be flowing in and out of the centre of his thought throughout the book.

Stephen, an elbow rested on the jagged granite, leaned his palm against his brow and gazed at the fraying edge of his shiny black coatsleeve. Pain, that was not yet the pain of love, fretted his heart. Silently, in a dream she had come to him after her death, her wasted body within its loose brown graveclothes giving off an odour of wax and rosewood, her breath,

78

that had bent upon him, mute, reproachful, a faint odour of wetted ashes. Across the threadbare cuffedge he saw the sea hailed as a great sweet mother by the wellfed voice beside him. The ring of bay and skyline held a dull green mass of liquid. A bowl of white china had stood beside her deathbed holding the green sluggish bile which she had torn up from her rotting liver by fits of loud groaning vomiting.

The nagging guilt, fretting at his heart, will be there all day, the "agenbite of inwit." And the word "rotting" that comes to him will run the range from decay and decomposition to putrescence. Two years have elapsed since Stephen announced in his journal, at the end of the *Portrait*, that he was going to "forge in the smithy of my soul the uncreated conscience of my race." He has not yet done this, but he will. He has lived and starved in Paris, a medical student, and memories of that residence mingle with his pre-medical studies in his reveries this June morning in Dublin:

My latin quarter hat. God, we simply must dress the character. I want puce gloves. You were a student, weren't you? Of what in the other devil's name? Paysayenn. P.C.N., you know: *physiques, chimiques et naturelles*. Aha.

He has returned hastily to Dublin, summoned by telegram, to the death-bed of his mother. Now there is guilt haunting him as a nagging hurt, a fantasy, a nightmare. The prayer he refused his mother runs recurrently through his mind.

Her glazing eyes, staring out of death, to shake and bend my soul. On me alone. The ghostcandle to light her agony. Ghostly light on the tortured face. Her hoarse loud breath rattling in horror, while all prayed on their knees. Her eyes on me to strike me down. *Liliata rutilantium te confessorum turma circumdet: iubilantium te virginum chorus excipiat.*
Ghoul! Chewer of corpses!
No, mother. Let me be and let me live.

Stephen is the same brilliant, arrogant, pedant-poet who gathers images from the whole reach of literature, who must transform and parody, whose genius can abstract a whole area of reference and allusion into a phrase and

79

whose mind must be used as an instrument of aggression against other minds. He decidedly is one who prepares a face to meet the faces that he meets, a man of brooding feeling and ashplant attitudes. A meeting with other minds is but an invitation to mental attack. "Unsheathe your dagger definitions." He will stab with definitions, with words.

—History, Stephen said, is a nightmare from which I am trying to awake.

From the playfield the boys raised a shout. A whirring whistle: goal. What if that nightmare gave you a back kick?

—The ways of the Creator are not our ways, Mr. Deasy said. All history moves towards one great goal, the manifestation of God.

Stephen jerked his thumb towards the window saying:

—That is God.

Hooray! Ay! Whrrhee!

—What? Mr. Deasy asked.

—A shout in the street, Stephen answered, shrugging his shoulders.

The shade of Vico presides over this conversation as A. M. Klein has brilliantly demonstrated. The shout in the street is but another manifestation of that original thunder that belonged to the Age of Gods; it is that lyric cry caught in a moment of time that rendered an emotion. But for us, in the mind of Stephen, it recalls the auditory sensibility of James Joyce, the near-sighted, for whom all Dublin is filled with shouts in the streets and voices, and in whose mind the older hurt of the punishment he unjustly received at Clongowes cannot be forgotten. Mingling with the guilt-theme of his mother's death, and a series of subsidiary themes, in the dissonant symphony of Stephen's mind, filled with contrasts of beauty and ugliness, little momentary occurrences serve as reminders of what has happened long before.

In the newspaper office, to which Dedalus goes to bring a letter written by his employer, the editor lays a hand on his shoulder:

—I want you to write something for me, he said. Something with a bite in it. You can do it. I see it in your face.

A memory is touched. The editor's words, "I see it in your face," belong far away to Stephen's past. He is in Clongowes Wood College again. The thought that now enters his mind is:

See it in your face. See it in your eye. Lazy idle little schemer.

The reader of *Ulysses* may wonder why Stephen thought of this. But if he has read *A Portrait of the Artist* he knows. There Father Dolan, prefect of studies, had punished Stephen unjustly: "Out here, Dedalus. Lazy little schemer. I see schemer in your face."

A few pages later in *Ulysses* Stephen is in the library stabbing in a number of directions with his dagger definitions. "Horseness is the whatness of allhorse. . . . God: noise in the street: very peripatetic. Space: what you damn well have to see." The phrase "agenbite of inwit" comes once more into his consciousness. He thinks of himself as ever-changing and wonders whether memory still makes him the same as before, when "I am other I now." He thinks of his student days, "I that sinned and prayed and fasted" and once again he soars back in time to Clongowes, "A child that Conmee saved from pandies." An allusion to Father Conmee, the rector, who assured him he would not be unjustly punished again.

These allusions to the episode in the *Portrait*, brief and fugitive, become an important episode of phantasmagoria in the night-town brothel scene three hundred pages farther on. Stephen lights a match, but is apparently too drunk to light his cigarette with it, for Lynch says to him: "You would have a better chance of lighting it if you held the match nearer." Stephen brings the match nearer to his eye and says or thinks:

Lynx eye. Must get glasses. Broke them yesterday. Sixteen years ago. Distance. The eye sees all flat. (*He draws the match away. It goes out.*) Brain thinks. Near: far. Ineluctable modality of the visible.

Clongowes and the broken glasses are again in Stephen's mind. Memory has come rushing in, and now it is sharpened by a series of associations arising directly from external stimuli. The cigarette slips from Stephen's fingers and he extends his hand to the harlot Zoë. She takes his hand and offers to read his palm. Stephen hears or imagines her saying, as she looks at his palm:

"I see it in your face. The eye, like that."

And at that moment Lynch slaps Kitty's buttocks twice; again Stephen's mind registers words either associated or actually heard: "Like that. Pandybat."

The combination of his extended palm and a slapping sound produces now the following images in fantasy, which Joyce renders (as he does this entire night-town scene, in a mixture of speech, thought, and stage directions, as if it were a play, or rather a scenario for a film):

(*Twice loudly a pandybat cracks, the coffin of the pianola flies open, the bald little round jack-in-the-box head of Father Dolan springs up.*

FATHER DOLAN

Any boy want flogging? Broke his glasses? Lazy idle little schemer. See it in your eye.

(*Mild, benign, rectorial, reproving, the head of Don John Conmee rises from the pianola coffin.*)

DON JOHN CONMEE

Now, Father Dolan! Now. I'm sure that Stephen's a very good little boy.

Only those who have read *A Portrait of the Artist as a Young Man* can understand the full meaning of this fantasy as it has arisen in Stephen's intoxicated mind. The cues which brought it out of his past were the words "I see it in your face" and the sound of the two slaps administered by Lynch to Kitty. We return to Clongowes Wood College, where Stephen Dedalus (in the *Portrait*) is a little boy, weak of sight. He has broken his glasses while running along the cinder-path. The prefect of studies enters the classroom and finds Stephen idle.

—Why is he not writing, Father Arnall?
—He broke his glasses, said Father Arnall, and I exempted him from work.
—Broke? What is this I hear? What is this? Your name is? said the prefect of studies.
—Dedalus, sir.

-Out here, Dedalus. Lazy little schemer. I see schemer in your face. Where did you break your glasses?

Stephen stumbled into the middle of the class, blinded by fear and haste.

—Where did you break your glasses? repeated the prefect of studies.

—The cinderpath, sir.

—Hoho! The cinderpath! cried the prefect of studies. I know that trick.

Stephen lifted his eyes in wonder and saw for a moment Father Dolan's whitegrey not young face, his baldy whitegrey head with fluff at the sides of it, the steel rims of his spectacles and his nocoloured eyes looking through the glasses. Why did he say he knew that trick?

—Lazy idle little loafer! cried the prefect of studies. Broke my glasses! An old schoolboy trick! Out with your hand this moment!

It is curious, however, to stumble upon other associations in Stephen's phantasmagoria in the night-town scene which take us back not to work commonly available to the public, like the *Portrait*, but to the early fragment, *Stephen Hero*, never intended for publication by Joyce. In this fragment Stephen says to his mother:

—It is a nice thing, that you go and discuss me behind my back. Have you not your own nature to guide you, your own sense of what is right, without going to some Father Jack-in-the-box to ask him to guide you?

Here then is the explanation of Father Dolan's "jack-in-the box" eruption from the pianola, and the synthesis here, if we examine all the elements that have become fused in Stephen's mind, is that of Mother Church and the mother Stephen defied on her death-bed and the guilt he feels and cannot banish; with this also, the memory of Father Dolan with his bald, round, jack-in-the-box head, who administered punishment to a near-sighted guiltless boy long before at Clongowes, and Stephen's years-long struggle with his waning faith. These are the tissues of past experience used by Stephen in his drunken dream-work during a trivial episode in a Dublin bawdy house.

The stream of consciousness of Leopold Bloom differs markedly from that of Stephen Dedalus, inevitably, since they are two quite different personalities. The type of mind Bloom has is not unlike that of Daniel Prince in *Les lauriers sont coupés*. He sees immediate images and reflects upon them immediately; he has a literal, fact-accumulating mind. He has absorbed all kinds of data and all manner of clichés. Through him we become aware of the city, in the concrete images it flashes into his mind. We accompany him as he fusses in the kitchen to make breakfast, as he buys the pork kidney, as he attends a funeral and meanders through Dublin's streets to the newspaper office, the library, to lunch, to his encounter with the irate Citizen. After other routine adventures of daily life he and Dedalus meet, drink together, and end up at the brothel.

Bloom's thoughts also have their leitmotiv. His mind keeps coming back during the day to the infidelities of his wife, to her affair with Blazes Boylan, to his own role as the cuckold. He is haunted also by the memory of his dead son, little Rudy, who died as a child and who will be identified at the end of the day with Stephen. Bloom is statistical (he is a solicitor of advertising) as we see him or his thoughts at Paddy Dignam's funeral:

Coffin now. Got here before us, dead as he is. Horse looking round at it with his plume skeowways. Dull eye: collar tight on his neck, pressing on a bloodvessel or something. Do they know what they cart out here every day? Must be twenty or thirty funerals every day. Then Mount Jerome for the protestants. Funerals all over the world everywhere every minute. Shovelling them under by the cartload doublequick. Thousands every hour. Too many in the world.

He experiences a wave of anxiety as the grave-diggers begin to fill the grave.

The gravediggers took up their spades and flung heavy clods of clay in on the coffin. Mr. Bloom turned his face. And if he was alive all the time? Whew! By Jingo, that would be awful! No, no: he is dead, of course. Of course he is dead. Monday he died. They ought to have some law to pierce the heart and make sure or an electric clock or a telephone in the coffin and some kind of canvas air-hole. Flag of distress. Three days. Rather long to keep them in summer. Just as well to get shut of them as soon as you are sure there's no.

The thought breaks here. Joyce intervenes as narrator to write "The clay fell softer." And Bloom's thoughts resume: "Begin to be forgotten. Out of sight, out of mind."

The worn-out phrase always serves to sum things up for Bloom. The established phrase has a finality that his own words cannot have. Experience for his consciousness leans heavily on the comfort of the familiar.

Mr. Bloom walked unheeded along his grove by saddened angels, crosses, broken pillars, family vaults, stone hopes praying with upcast eyes, old Ireland's hearts and hands. More sensible to spend the money on some charity for the living. Pray for the repose of the soul of. Does anybody really? Plant him and have done with him. Like down a coalshoot. Then lump them together to save time. All souls' day.

From the moment he gives Marion or Molly Bloom a letter and sees her tuck it hastily under the pillow he knows that she is planning to see Blazes Boylan. All that day he tries to push this out of his mind. Little incidents, however—fragments of song, a walk past a theatre, a chance remark—act as cues to force it back into the centre of consciousness. Boylan has been trying to arrange a series of concerts for the musical Mrs Bloom. Early in the book Bloom looks at the playbills outside the Queen's Theatre, a series of coming events, and thinks: "He's coming in the afternoon. Her songs." Sixty pages later in Davy Byrne's, where Bloom has retreated for a sandwich, Nosey Flynn asks him about his wife's concert tour and who is getting it up. Bloom avoids answering. Then Flynn interjects: "Isn't Blazes Boylan mixed up in it?"

A warm shock of air heat of mustard haunched on Mr Bloom's heart. He raised his eyes and met the stare of a bilious clock. Two. Pub clock five minutes fast. Time going on. Hands moving. Two. Not yet.

In the brothel the day's little interspaced thoughts and anxieties merge into a vast fantasy of Marion and Blazes,

85

and Bloom listens to the timepiece, sounding "Cuckoo" thrice and "the brass quoits of a bed are heard to jingle."

Stephen walks through Dublin haunted by the memory of a dead mother and his guilt. Bloom is haunted by the hurt and mortification of the cuckold. He has been described as *l'homme moyen sensuel*, but he has, as Lenehan remarks in the pub scene, "a touch of the artist" about him. His thoughts are staccato. The immediate Dublin scene mingles with his inner wounds; and into his stream of thought come scraps of memory from the European ghettoes—for Bloom in Dublin is Odysseus the wanderer and also the Wandering Jew. And his sense of exile has its spiritual counterpart in Stephen's feeling of homelessness as an artist, even though, unlike Bloom, he is in his homeland. Stephen has spoken of Ireland as "an afterthought of Europe." The Wandering Jew can be identified also as an "afterthought"—and, in the eyes of the nations, as an historic superfluity.

Bloom's mind is a pastiche of Dublin and of history. It is a rag-bag of the sentimental and the maudlin. He is alternately a functioning animal and a man with certain intellectual pretensions, yet without any curiosity. He can explain the meaning of "metempsychosis" to his illiterate wife not through any sensitivity to words but because he is a reader of "fact" magazines. He has a newspaper mind. He is gross, sensual. He loves the innards of animals; at the same time he is an affectionate man and a lover of animals.

The cat walked stiffly round a leg of the table with tail on high.
—Mkgnao!
—O, there you are, Mr Bloom said, turning from the fire.
The cat mewed in answer and stalked again stiffly round a leg of the table, mewing. Just how she stalks over my writing-table. Prr. Scratch my head. Prr.
Mr Bloom watched curiously, kindly, the lithe black form. Clean to see: the gloss of her sleek hide, the white button under the butt of her tail, the green flashing eyes. He bent down to her, his hands on his knees.
—Milk for the pussens, he said.
—Mrkgnao! the cat cried.

86

They call them stupid. They understand what we say better
than we understand them. She understands all she wants to.
Vindictive too. Wonder what I look like to her. Height of a
tower? No, she can jump me.
—Afraid of the chickens she is, he said mockingly. Afraid of
the chookchooks. I never saw such a stupid pussens as the
pussens.
Cruel. Her nature. Curious mice never squeal. Seem to like
it.
—Mrkrgnao! the cat said loudly.
She blinked up out of her avid shameclosing eyes, mewing
plaintively and long, showing him her milkwhite teeth.

In the brothel scene Bloom's consciousness, like Dedalus's, is dramatized in a series of visions, a jumble of
thoughts and images, described sometimes as stage directions, sometimes in speech which may not be speech so
much as thought. It is written in a manner recalling
Flaubert's *Temptation of St Anthony*. Bloom fancies himself
in the brothel in many roles, ranging from a criminal,
punished for being a cuckold, and a pander, to the most
exalted being in Europe:

A BLACKSMITH

(*Murmurs*) For the Honour of God! And is that Bloom? He
scarcely looks thirtyone.

A PAVIOR AND FLAGGER

That's the famous Bloom now, the world's greatest reformer.
Hats off!

(*All uncover their heads. Women whisper eagerly.*)

A MILLIONAIRESS

(*Richly.*) Isn't he simply wonderful?

A NOBLEWOMAN

(*Nobly.*) All that man has seen!

A FEMINIST

(*Masculinely.*) And done!

A BELLHANGER

A classic face! He has the forehead of a thinker.

(*Bloom's weather. A sunburst appears in the northwest.*)

THE BISHOP OF DOWN AND CONNOR

I here present your undoubted emperor president and king
chairman, the most serene and potent and very puissant ruler
of this realm. God save Leopold the First!

We are now in the consciousness of Leopold the First as he begins to bestow largesse. In this scene and throughout the *Walpurgisnacht* episode, James Joyce has reached far beyond the simple straight line of thought we find in Dorothy Richardson or in *A Portrait of the Artist*. He has tried to catch—and to a marked degree has succeeded—the phantasmagoria of consciousness as well.

4

What shall we say of the stream of consciousness of Marion Tweedy Bloom, that long, rambling, unpunctuated (but paragraphed), silent monologue with which the book ends? It is perhaps no longer a stream but a torrent, a *tour de force* of invention and ingenuity, and certainly one of the most striking portions of the book. We have seen little of Marion Bloom during the day, but have felt her presence in the continuing fantasies of her husband. In the morning we caught a glimpse of her as Leopold served her breakfast in bed.

—What a time you were, she said.

She set the brasses jingling as she raised herself briskly, an elbow on the pillow. He looked calmly down on her bulk and between her large soft bubs, sloping within her nightdress like a shegoat's udder. The warmth of her couched body rose on the air, mingling with the fragrance of the tea she poured.

Then she starts searching through a book for a word she has encountered.

—Here, she said. What does that mean?

He leaned downward and read near her polished thumbnail. . . .

—Metempsychosis, he said, frowning. It's Greek: from the Greek. That means the transmigration of souls.

—O, rocks! she said. Tell us in plain words.

Molly has in this way been briefly characterized for us. Later we glimpse only her arm, emerging from the window, as she drops a coin to a one-legged sailor during the Dublin panorama scene. She will describe herself at the end of the book in the language of her mind.

We enter her mind when Bloom's wanderings during

his Dublin day come to their end. He has brought Stephen home and sobered him up. Stephen has left, and Bloom goes to bed announcing to Molly that next morning she must bring him his breakfast. At that moment we are introduced into her consciousness. Her thoughts come closest in the book to what we have described as "internal monologue." Her memories enfold one another; involuntary associations arise, provoking others. She is in bed beside her husband and there are virtually no external stimuli to provoke their own associations. Only at one or two points do such stimuli intrude into her flow of thought: a train screeching through the night, "train somewhere whistling the strength those engines have in them like big giants" (Mrs Bloom likes big strong things), then a few pages later a thought, "I can see his face clean shaven," is interrupted by "that train again." On the next page a final allusion "there's that train far away."

She seems on the whole unmindful of Bloom's presence in the bed beside her, although he is in and out of her thoughts constantly, and we gather she has been listening to him snore, for we get, "O move over your big carcass out of that for the love of Mike listen to him." The state in which Joyce gives us Molly's consciousness is similar to that in which the psycho-analyst often prefers to have his patient, so that the associations may flow freely and without interruption of external stimuli—the couch, the soundless room, the supine position. We are largely in the centre of Molly's thoughts, and for this reason the technique used by Joyce in this portion of *Ulysses* is less revolutionary than it seems. Only the absence of punctuation and of inhibition give the reader the sense of mental flow and of being an eye-witness to the unharnessed libido of Molly Bloom.

It is not the technique that is bold here so much as the attempt on the part of a male writer to convey the *inner* consciousness of a woman. Women writers have *described* men, and male writers women, but the description has usually been external. When Henry James wrote *The Portrait of a Lady* several women writers raised their eyebrows in surprise, and one complimented him on his audacity in essaying to penetrate and convey the inner being of Isabel Archer. Dorothy Richardson's work was begun precisely because she felt that in most novels the reader moved in a male world, and she was determined to leave a record of the female consciousness. But it was Joyce who performed the creative feat of rendering Marion Tweedy Bloom almost wholly from within.

Nevertheless, the question still remains whether Mrs Bloom is not in reality a masculine concept of what the feminine mind might be, and the sexuality with which Joyce endows Mrs Bloom may have in it—particularly in its active tone—much more masculine imagination than feminine feeling. For Rebecca West at least, the fantasies of Mrs Bloom's mind seem to lack conviction in the light of her quite satisfactory sexual encounter that afternoon with Blazes Boylan. Her accumulation of sexual day-dream, much of it aggressive, would be better explained, Miss West observes, in someone undergoing "the torments of abstinence."

Such arguments simplify the problem unduly. There are in both sexes sufficient awareness of the opposite sex and components of masculinity and femininity in greater or lesser degree which enable the artist to paint men and women as they are. The question for criticism is the degree of their success. The writer of stream of consciousness has, after all, been inside no mind but his own, and it is the measure of his daring that he seeks to convey the atmosphere of many other minds—Joyce that of an erotic and earthy woman, Faulkner even that of an imbecile.

5

At the end of the day in Dublin we know Stephen, Leopold, and Molly more intimately than most other characters in fiction; and yet for some readers they may not be as palpable as say Becky Sharp or Emma Bovary. This might be because we have had very little chance to see Joyce's characters from the outside—to get off at a sufficient distance to take a good look at the fleshly appearance of them. Nor have we seen them together, save during the brief passage in the brothel, when Stephen and

Leopold meet, and the subsequent long chapter in the cab-man's shelter and the chapter of catechism. There, however, they are both drunk and lost in their separate worlds. Mrs Bloom's internal monologue is isolated at the end of the book. There is no doubt that Joyce by this means accentuates to a remarkable degree our sense of the way in which individuals move in their own envelope of consciousness, isolated and undivined. But the reader, moving with them and experiencing them, does have a picture of their lives and their lonely journeys—lonely sometimes even when most gregarious—through the world-city of Dublin.

What are the essential differences between the consciousness of Dedalus and of Bloom? The difference, markedly established, seems to me to be that between the individual who abstracts and synthesizes experience, as Stephen the poet does, and the individual who is a mere receptacle and tabulator of perceptions and sensations, registering them now blurred, now sharp, but generally passive. By this means the inner difference in the texture of the two minds is established. The minds correspond completely to the different personalities Joyce is trying to create.

Wyndham Lewis has complained that the stream-of-consciousness writer "robs work of all linear properties whatsoever, of all contour and definition . . . the romantic abdominal *within* method results in a jellyfish structure, without articulation of any sort." This judgment takes stock of the intellectual rather than emotional content of consciousness. It might be applied to some extent to Dorothy Richardson, in whose work the consciousness of Miriam is in itself the subject of the work. In *Ulysses*, where the subject is the day in Dublin, there is careful articulation and focusing of the stream of consciousness of the three principal characters. Far from being just a mass of musical notations all chords and dissonances, there is a thematic structure one might describe as symphonic, which provides distinct "linear properties" over and above the Homeric frame upon which Joyce constructed his book. Stephen's thoughts take structure around his guilt-problem, and Bloom's flow from the domestic situation in Eccles Street.

The musical structure of *Ulysses* and the music of *Finnegans Wake* take us back not only to Joyce's own musical training and his aural sensitivity—he had hoped to become a professional singer—but again to the theories of the symbolists. Dujardin always said that Wagner was the main source of inspiration for the internal monologue in *Les lauriers sont coupés*, equating the themes which the mind calls up recurrently in the form of memories with the flowing Wagnerian label-themes.

One of the most illuminating episodes of Joyce's middle years was his espousal in Paris of the cause of his fellow-countryman, the tenor Sullivan. The Irish singer had difficulty in obtaining bookings at the Paris Opera, although he was the only singer then available who could reach all the high notes in *William Tell* and *Les Huguenots*, operas that were being revived that year. Whenever Sullivan did get a chance to appear, Joyce led a claque to the opera. His "bravo, bravo" seemed to hit the great chandelier and, echoing through the opera house, was the signal for applause. "Sullivan sings 45 G's, 93 A flats, 92 A's, 54 B flats, 15 B's, 19 C's, and two C sharps," Joyce exulted after examining the score of *William Tell*. The novelist was offering statistics in the manner of Leopold Bloom; but it was also Joyce, the Irish tenor, who had become a writer instead of a singer, admiring the performance of a fellow-virtuoso. Since thoughts repeat themselves in different forms and recur at irregular intervals, unpredictable and involuntary, by a process of association, they constituted themselves for James Joyce as the recurring notes of a musical score, a kind of music of the mind. Memorable in *Ulysses* is the long chapter written in fugal structure, set in Ormond's Bar, where the themes enunciated at the beginning are developed note by note amid the drinking, the hubbub, the clinking of glasses, the sounds and voices and snatches of song, while bronze by gold, Miss Douce's head by Miss Kennedy's, the barmaids float in and out of sound, two islands of colour.

From the moment the artist attempts to render the music of the mind, the counterpoint of consciousness, as Joyce did, he is caught up as we have seen in the Here and the Now "through which all future plunges to the past." Consciousness, however, does not measure time by mechanical means. It possesses its own time-measure, different within each individual. The psychological novelist must actively concern himself, accordingly, with psychological time.

CHAPTER VIII

THE ARBITRARY DIAL: EPIPHANY

THE NOVELS we have been discussing have been called by some critics "time-novels." Certainly *time* might be said to be their primary concern. We have seen how in *Ulysses* Joyce was preoccupied with the preservation, in words, of eighteen hours of experience, retrieved so to speak from all eternity. So Marcel Proust's quest for "lost time" is an attempt on an heroic scale to recapture the memories of moments that have long disappeared but which still live somewhere in the consciousness. These, too, may be preserved in an enduring mould of words. Proust spoke of his wish to "seize, isolate, immobilize for the duration of a lightning flash . . . a fragment of pure time in its pure state." Dostoevsky expressed an analogous wish when he described the heightening of sensory experience—the "aura"—just before an epileptic seizure, and remarked that he would have given years of his life to live through a few such moments gathered together and made continuous. Virginia Woolf recurs constantly to "the moment" which, like Blake's grain of sand, can hold a world within its fractional pulse—the very incandescence of consciousness. And William Faulkner, coming after these explorers, wrote into the core of his work the meaning of the "arbitrary dial," whose shadow marks the Present and absorbs also all that is Past.

The face of the mechanical clock stares at us from these novels: we hear the hours ticking, bells ring, clocks chime, Big Ben's bronze syllables float through the London air, and in the Dublin of Joyce's discarded fragment, *Stephen Hero*, young Dedalus looks upon the face of the clock and experiences—an epiphany!

He told Cranly that the clock of the Ballast Office was capable of an epiphany. Cranly questioned the inscrutable dial of the Ballast Office with his no less inscrutable countenance:

94

--Yes, said Stephen, I will pass it time after time, allude to it, refer to it, catch a glimpse of it. It is only an item in the catalogue of Dublin's street furniture. Then all at once I see it and I know at once what it is: epiphany.

—What?

—Imagine my glimpse at that clock as the gropings of a spiritual eye which seeks to adjust its vision to an exact focus. The moment the focus is reached the object is epiphanised.

By an "epiphany" he meant "a sudden spiritual manifestation, whether in the vulgarity of speech or in a memorable phrase of the mind itself." And the young Dedalus believed that "it was for the man of letters to record these epiphanies with extreme care seeing that they themselves are the most delicate and evanescent of moments." Although Joyce discarded the term in the final form of the *Portrait*, he defines very carefully in that book—with the aid of St Thomas Aquinas—the aesthetic experience implicit in his concept of the artist's epiphany: isolation of the given image from its surroundings—*integritas*; perception of formal harmony in it—*consonantia*; and the emotional content of the experience—*claritas*. The process is often simultaneous, in an instant of perception, that instant when "the clear radiance of the aesthetic image is apprehended luminously by the mind which has been arrested by its wholeness and fascinated by its harmony." In this lies the "silent stasis of aesthetic pleasure" Joyce visioned as a spiritual state (hence the original term "epiphany"), what Galvani called the "enchantment of the heart."

Joyce here is describing in reality the functioning of the creative imagination: what occurs in an artist's mind before he begins the difficult act of recording and communicating his experience. The novelist was aware, however, that much of what he imaginatively experienced could be recorded only in the most approximate way, by use of symbols, and that what would be communicated—if anything—might be largely an atmosphere and a state of feeling, as complex and subjective in the reader as in the experience of the writer. When Joyce described Verlaine's poems as "remote from conscious purpose as rain

95

that falls in a garden . . . the rhythmic speech of an emotion otherwise incommunicable," he was suggesting— with the symbolists—that in literature words and symbols alone can communicate, in the most general fashion and largely atmospherically, emotions that otherwise defy both rendering and communication. Stephen Dedalus asks himself: "Did he then love the rhythmic rise and fall of words better than their associations of legend and colour?" Joyce, as the world was to discover, began by loving words in this way but ultimately sought to make them convey the legends and associations they symbolized, as well as the colours and tones they suggested, to his imagination. Sounds, words, like thoughts, are experienced in time and they have been, from primitive days, man's means of giving vocal expression to emotion.

The lyrical form is in fact the simplest verbal vesture of an instant of emotion, a rhythmical cry such as ages ago cheered on the man who pulled at the oar or dragged stones up a slope. He who utters it is more conscious of the instant of emotion than of himself as feeling emotion.

Finnegans Wake is already upon the horizon. While Joyce seized upon the visual, the palpable in experience, he sought, with perhaps the most sensitive ear in English literature since Shakespeare and Milton, to render that which was audible as well. Stephen at one moment in *Ulysses* equates a shout in the street with God, thus suggesting the spiritual qualities Joyce felt in this synthesis by which the audible or the visible or both—time or space or again both—merge in the artist's consciousness to form his "instant of emotion" or epiphany.

The psychological novelist attempts to arrest a moment of time at every step even as it flees before him. He may contemplate a statue, a picture, a landscape, a city, for hours: always the form of what is being viewed remains reasonably fixed and recognizable. But the instant of emotion, the moment of perception, the shout in the street, the epiphany—these are heard and are gone, the moment flames brightly and becomes a fading coal. How arrest this kinetic moment of the mind? How give it the

96

static quality possessed by a statue? This was at the heart of Joyce's problem—and the problem of those who followed in his footsteps. When she was at work on *To the Lighthouse* Virginia Woolf set down these lines in her diary:

I am now and then haunted by some semi-mystic very profound life of a woman, which shall all be told on one occasion; and time shall be utterly obliterated; future shall somehow blossom out of the past. One incident—say the fall of a flower —might contain it. My theory being that the actual event practically does not exist—nor time either.

The "slice of life" of the nineteenth-century realists here becomes the "slice of time." From trying to capture "the moment"—say the fall of a flower—the artist begins to question whether the moment ever existed. Only he knows that it does exist—as a kind of eternal present.

2

This intense awareness of time as a merging of time past and time present, as T. S. Eliot has put it,

Time past and time future
What might have been and what has been
Point to one end, which is always present,

is at the very core of the work of William Faulkner. Proust's awareness resided in his aching need to recover the past; Faulkner's arose from his having grown up in a society in which the past had virtually engulfed the present. A South in which the Civil War exists as a contemporary reality in the minds of young men who listen largely to talk of the Long Before; in which animosities have never been extinguished and old feelings continue to bubble and to rage, is very like Faulkner's Benjy, who has been three years old for thirty years. There is no dividing line between what is and what was in Benjy's retarded consciousness, no distinction between an immediate reality and memory. Reverend Hightower, preaching fervently to his flock, could still hear the clatter of horses' hooves and see the great swirl of dust of the old war, although he was born after the struggle; and Sam Fathers, telling young McCaslin stories of a family past, made them seem in the present:

And as he talked about those old times and those dead and vanished men of another race from either that the boy knew, gradually to the boy those old times would cease to be old times and would become a part of the boy's present, not only as if they had happened yesterday but as if they were still happening, the men who walked through them actually walking in breath and air and casting an actual shadow on the earth they had not quitted.

William Faulkner, who had been transported from the New World to the Old as an aviator of the First World War, had ample opportunity to observe this strange process: in Oxford, Mississippi, he had become aware of the melting together of the Old South and the New and seen how legends persist long after their creators are gone. Legend has it he was stationed at Oxford, England. For him the two Oxfords, each encased in its own long tradition, could melt together even as the American recovers in England certain elements of his own past and present. Indeed the new war could melt into the old. And so, too, the story of Calvary had become timeless and had been enacted anew, while being a repetition of what had happened before.

The structure and content of Faulkner's masterpiece, *The Sound and the Fury*, can be understood only if we grasp his singular absorption with time—or timelessness. On the surface it appears to be a story of the three Compson sons, told to us through their stream of consciousness on three different days. In this process, however, we become acquainted with the decay of the Compson family, and by the same token of the American South. We observe, and are made to feel, the swallowing up of the present by the past.

As Cranly, in Joyce's fragment, questions "the inscrutable dial of the Ballast Office," Quentin Compson questions the "round stupid assertion of the clock." He, however, wants to wipe it out of existence. If time could stand still he would not have to die. Having fixed the hour for his suicide, he can live only by annihilating time. He tears the hands off his father's watch (which was also his grand-father's), but the ticking does not cease. (So the South had torn the hands of time without shutting out its inexorable tick.) His father had told him that clocks slay time and had given him the ancestral watch, "not that you may remember time, but that you might forget it now and then for a moment, and not spend all your breath trying to conquer it." Nevertheless, Quentin spends the last day of his life in a kind of time-rage trying to conquer it. In tearing the hands off the watch he seeks to obliterate the present. Obliteration of the present, however, is a denial of life.

And life refuses to be denied. The sun pursues its course, shadows lengthen, time-whistles blow, the "staring eyes" of clocks are encountered. These may be contradictory and confusing, as Quentin, leaving the jewellery store discovers:

I went out, shutting the door upon the ticking. I looked back into the window. . . . There were about a dozen watches in the window, a dozen different hours and each with the same assertive and contradictory assurance that mine had, without any hands at all. Contradicting one another. I could hear mine, ticking away inside my pocket, even though nobody could see it, even though it could tell nothing if anyone could.

But it ticks on to sunset. The day does have an ending. So Quentin destroys himself, in reality because he has been unable to put the present into meaningful relation with the past.

Jason, the Compson who seems at first glance to be completely in touch with reality, deploys a vast surface energy in acting out his hatred of his fellow-men and in hoarding petty sums. His father had urged his sons not to "spend all your breath" trying to conquer time. Jason is always breathless. He knows only mechanical time; he runs in his little maze and cannot stop running. He is nearly always late, and all the while he strains to be on time. His time-sense is as faulty as Quentin's, but at the opposite extreme. He knows only the inching present, as Quentin knew only an engulfing past. All he achieves is

99

a constant self-frustration. The present has trapped him in a chamber a few city blocks long. As Quentin sought to forget the present, so Jason is incapable of forgetting it. Time for both is an unsorted jumble.*

We have already alluded to Benjy, the third Compson, for whom time has no boundaries and whose imbecile consciousness remembers only by blurred associations: he is thirty-three at one moment, thirteen at another. And suddenly he is a boy of five. Experience is all one, names and places cannot be distinguished from one another, the entire world moves around him comfortable when familiar, anxiety-provoking when unfamiliar. He can hear the dark; the spoon "came up and I ate" and "the bowl steamed up to my face." The lawn comes to him and goes away. Benjy lives in a world of presence and absence, of immediate sensations that are also past sensations. Faulkner has created him in a vein of compassionate poetry, making of him a kind of repository of all the emotional chaos of the Compsons.

In the Compson household only one person has a firm grip on time and, by this token, on reality. This is Dilsey, the Negro cook. She is aware that the clock of the South lags. She knows that for the Negro in the South there is always a difference in time. To the chiming of the Compson family clock she listens attentively. She counts its hours. Then she adds three more.

Faulkner boldly violated chronological sequence in *The Sound and the Fury*, perhaps in imitation of the human consciousness itself. The mind cannot accommodate itself to chronological or mechanical time, but is constantly moving blocks of time from past-to-present-to-past, and without regard for logical sequence. In doing this the American novelist showed how completely he had grasped the essential characteristic of the psychological novel. The time of the book covers only four days—the three days of the three brothers plus Dilsey's day—yet it covers the entire emotional history of the Compson family (which is

* See Perrin Lowrey's admirable discussion of this in "Concepts of Time in *The Sound and the Fury*," in *English Institute Essays* (New York 1954).

also the emotional history of the South). We are in Benjy's mind on 7 April, 1928. We are in Quentin Compson's mind, during the second section, eighteen years *earlier*, 2 June, 1910, the day he drowned himself. We are in Jason Compson's mind 6 April, 1928, the day *before* we were in Benjy's mind. And in the final section the omniscient author returns to the scene to tell us in conventional fashion the events of 8 April, 1928, Dilsey's day—the day *after* the Benjy section. Only when we have read the entire book is it possible to unscramble the time-element and allow all the data to fall into place in our mind. The problems involved in reading *The Sound and the Fury* are not unlike those discussed earlier in connection with Dorothy Richardson, with this significant difference: in Miss Richardson's work we were sorting out the data furnished us by one mind, whereas here we have, by the end of the book, lived through three highly dissimilar minds and discovered how they were related to a common family experience. In making us aware of the disordered time-sense of real life, that is of psychological time, Faulkner not only dramatised for us the three minds and the confusion of time that exists in memory, but heightened our awareness of the depths of mental experience. At the same time his book serves to dramatise the fact that when a novelist takes us into the minds of his characters he can no longer remain in an historical past, seeking out for us a story of what *has* happened. He must confront us with what *is* happening at the very moment that Quentin is smashing the face of his father's watch, or Big Ben is chiming 11 a.m. for Mrs Dalloway, or the clocks in Oxford Street are pointing to 1.30 p.m. for Hugh Whitbread. And this points to the larger goal of the psychological novelist, exemplified in Proust and his search for time past and "pure time"—his sense that the chiming and ticking are constant reminders of an ebbing time in a consciousness that in reality lives only in a momentary present, an endless past. This larger goal is to enshrine experience and thereby render it impervious to time.

The accretion of historical and geographical memory that the two Oxfords symbolize in the biography of

William Faulkner—evident to a marked degree in his re-telling as a fable for our time of the Christ story—was what James Joyce tried to record in a different way in *Ulysses* and *Finnegans Wake*. Each in their own way, the Irish writer and the American who followed him, arrived at a vision of mental experience as something overlaid with a multitude of meanings, and each crystallised in his art the richness of that experience.

In *Ulysses* Joyce had demonstrated how the seemingly "jellyfish" material of consciousness could be used to expand one of his epiphanies into a great picture of a single day in a teeming city. In *The Sound and the Fury*, by taking us into three minds, Faulkner made us aware of the tragedy of the South. In both these works the streams of consciousness were poured into a series of moulds; yet for all their moulding, the thoughts and sensations of each consciousness portrayed had to be assimilated by the consciousness of the reader. The interesting critical problem that we may now formulate is this: however ingenious and however different the portrayal of the three streams of consciousness in *Ulysses* and in *The Sound and the Fury*, they each spring in reality from a single stream of consciousness, that is the mind and being of James Joyce or William Faulkner. In other words: Is the creation of off-shoots of a consciousness—however rich the off-shoots—in essence a form of autobiography, the emptying of the artist's minds to artistic ends? This is the all-but-final step in our inquiry.

CHAPTER IX

THE NOVEL AS AUTOBIOGRAPHY

IN *Honeycomb*, the third chapter or volume of her *Pilgrimage*, Dorothy Richardson's heroine, Miriam Henderson, makes a discovery while she is reading a book. It is that "I don't read books for the story, but as a psychological study of the author." Books come to mean to her "not the people in the books, but knowing, absolutely, everything about the author. . . . In life everything was so scrappy and mixed up. In a book the author was there in every word."

She embroiders this. "If only she could make Eve see what a book was . . . a dance by the author, a song, a prayer, an important sermon, a message. Books were not stories printed on paper, they were people; the real people."

In Virginia Woolf's early novel, *The Voyage Out*, a character, talking about his unwritten novels, says, "All you read a novel for is to see what sort of person the writer is, and, if you know him, which of his friends he's put in. As for the novel itself, the whole conception, the way one's seen the thing, felt about it, made it stand in relation to other things, not one in a million cares for that."

Criticism, of course, does care. And the problem that arises, particularly in the psychological novel, is whether we do not have so much more of the writer than in the conventional novel—since he has, so to speak, emptied the contents of his inner self for us. "The danger," wrote Virginia Woolf in her diary in 1920, "is the damned egotistical self; which ruins Joyce and Richardson to my mind: is one pliant and rich enough to provide a wall for the book from oneself without its becoming, as in Joyce and Richardson, narrowing and restricting?" She was writing, indeed, before she had read all of *Ulysses*. But the problem she stated was concrete enough. Does the psychological novelist write *fiction*, in the fullest sense of the word, or the book of himself? Is it possible to provide the "wall for the book from oneself" that Virginia Woolf would have liked to erect?

I

During the last year of his life Marcel Proust was asked by the journal *Les Annales* to discuss the distinction between the analytical novel and the adventure novel. He replied that the expression "analytical novel" was not to his taste. It had come to mean, he said, a study under a microscope, and he added, "the instrument I prefer is the telescope." He went on:

I was unfortunate enough to start a book with the word, "I," and immediately it was assumed that instead of trying to discover universal laws, I was "analysing myself," in the personal and odious sense of the word. I shall, therefore, if you are willing, replace the term "analytical novel" by "introspective novel."

After discussing adventure novels, he went on to say that the introspective novel must not be a novel of pure intellect.

It has to do with drawing a reality out of the unconscious in such a way as to make it enter into the realm of the intellect, while trying to preserve its life, not to garble it, to subject it to the least possible shrinkage—a reality which the light of intellect alone would be enough to destroy, so it seems. To succeed in this work of salvage, all the forces of the mind, and even of the body, are not superfluous. It is a little like the cautious, docile, intrepid effort necessary to someone who, while still asleep, would like to explore his sleep with his mind without this intervention leading to his awakening. His precautions must be taken. But although it apparently embodies a contradiction, this form of work is not impossible.

It *was* possible. Proust himself demonstrated this, as the sixteen volumes published by Gallimard show. What Proust is saying about trying to discover the nature of sleep without waking up is akin to what William James said when he spoke of turning up the gas to discover what the darkness is like. Proust believed, however, that in that fragment of a fragment of a second, in which the gas begins to cast its light into the darkness, the precious moment of pure time can be caught in static form. How difficult that is, we may judge from the fact that it took all Proust's energies and his whole life to arrive at a few such fragments of experience, and this by the process not of the *immediate* capturing and recording of the epiphany, but by the slow, deep, search of memory through film upon film of association.

It may seem whimsical and perverse for a novelist, as addicted to analysing a moment as we would analyse a year, to invoke the telescope rather than the microscope. Yet Proust was being perfectly honest. His purpose, as we know, was a search for universal laws, for Time—not the time which we see ticking its way mechanically across the face of a clock, but that Time which sometimes makes five minutes seem like a day, and makes a day sometimes pass as if it were five minutes.

Henry James, sitting down to write the first volume of his memoirs, *A Small Boy and Others*, used a phrase on the very first page that showed him—engaged as he was in the process of writing autobiography—to be starting with the same essential purpose as Proust (and it was at the same time, also, for James's first volume was published in 1913, the year of *Swann's Way*). He speaks on the first page of "my interrogation of the past." This could be a way of freely translating *À la recherche du temps perdu*. "It was to memory in the first place," said James, "that my main appeal for particulars had to be made."

We have thus exemplified here, in the one case in an autobiography and in the other in a novel that appears to be thinly disguised autobiography, the working of the same process. Memory and association—the word "association" flowers on page after page of James's memoirs—are the primary source of autobiography as they are of fiction. This, however, is a very bald and quite unsubtle statement of a matter infinitely complex.

To understand better the relationship between autobiography and the novel let us look briefly into the texture of the memories invoked by the two writers. Here is a small boy remembering his love of the theatre:

Every morning I would hasten to the Moriss column to see what new plays it announced. Nothing could be more disinterested or happier than the dreams with which these announcements filled my mind, dreams which took their form from the inevitable associations of the words forming the title of the play, and also from the colour of the bills, still damp and wrinkled with paste, on which those words stood out. Nothing, unless it were such strange titles as the *Testament de César Girodot* or *Œdipe-Roi*, inscribed not on the green bills of the Opéra-Comique, but on the wine-coloured bills of the Comédie-Française, nothing seemed to me to differ more profoundly from the sparkling white plume of the *Diamants de la Couronne* than the sleek, mysterious satin of the *Domino Noir*.

And here is another small boy remembering:

There were finer vibrations as well—for the safely-prowling infant, though none perhaps so fine as when he stood long and drank deep at those founts of romance that gushed from the huge placards of the theatre. These announcements, at a day when advertisement was contentedly but information, had very much the form of magnified play-bills; they consisted of vast oblong sheets, yellow or white, pasted upon tall wooden screens or into hollow sockets, and acquainting the possible playgoer with every circumstance that might seriously interest him. These screens rested sociably against trees and lamp-posts as well as against walls and fences, to all of which they were, I suppose, familiarly attached; but the sweetest note of their confidence was that, in parallel lines and the good old way, characters facing performers, they gave the whole cast, which in the "palmy days" of the drama often involved many names. I catch myself again in the fact of endless stations in Fifth Avenue near the south-west corner of Ninth Street, as I think it must have been, since the dull long "run" didn't exist then for the young *badaud* and the poster there was constantly and bravely renewed. It engaged my attention, whenever I passed, as the canvas of a great master in a great gallery holds that of the pious tourist, and even though I can't at this day be sure of its special reference I was with precocious passion "at home" among the theatres.

The seventy-year-old man remembering the precocious passion of the small boy in New York for the theatre was perhaps less addicted to searching for the finer mental *odour* of his experience than the middle-aged man in the cork-lined room looking at his boyhood self before the playbills of the Théâtre-Français. Yet both were writing curiously similar autobiography and each for a different end. In the case of Henry James it was for the pleasure of studying the growth of an imagination, *his* imagination. In the case of Proust it was to carry out a process of remembering, to discover the very nature of memory. Nevertheless, there are many significant parallels to be discerned in these dissimilar works. Perhaps this shows how similar the interests and awarenesses of small sensitive boys may be even in cultures and cities as removed from each other and as different as New York and Paris:

Upon the permanent foundation of eggs, cutlets, potatoes, preserves, and biscuits, whose appearance on the table she no longer announced to us, Françoise would add—as the labour of fields and orchards, the harvest of the tides, the luck of the markets, the kindness of neighbours, and her own genius might provide; and so effectively that our bill of fare, like the quatrefoils that were carved on the porches of cathedrals in the thirteenth century, reflected to some extent the march of the seasons and the incidents of human life—a brill, because the fish-woman had guaranteed its freshness; a turkey, because she had seen a beauty in the market at Roussainville-le-Pin; cardoons with marrow, because she had never done them for us in that way before; a roast leg of mutton, because the fresh air made one hungry and there would be plenty of time for it to "settle down" in the seven hours before dinner; spinach, by way of a change; apricots, because they were still hard to get; gooseberries, because in another fortnight there would be none left; raspberries, which M. Swann had brought specially; cherries, the first to come from the cherry-tree, which had yielded none for the last two years; a cream cheese, of which in those days I was extremely fond; an almond cake, because she had ordered one the evening before; a fancy loaf, because it was our turn to "offer" the holy bread. And when all these had been eaten, a work composed expressly for ourselves, but dedicated more particularly to my father, who had a fondness for such things, a cream of chocolate, inspired in the mind, created by the hand of Françoise, would be laid before us, light and fleeting as an "occasional piece" of music, into which she had poured the whole of her talent.

The boy in New York did not have as refined a palate. Nothing as fine as the *omelette aux tomates* and bottle of straw-coloured Chablis that Lambert Strether and Madame de Vionnet consume in *The Ambassadors* is evoked in *A Small Boy and Others*. The memories, nevertheless, are of a distinctly American palate, ice-cream consumed at every turn, hot cakes and sausages flooded with molasses on the hospitable porch of some Southern neighbours who settled in Fourteenth Street, doughnuts on Broadway, and waffles by the hundred, "the oblong farinaceous compound, faintly yet richly brown, stamped and smoking, not crisp nor brittle, but softly absorbent of the syrup dabbed upon it," and then peaches! Ah, the peaches *d'antan*! The small boy remembered certain "capital peach trees" in his grandmother's back yard in Albany and peaches on the New York water-front,

> Bushels of peaches in particular, peaches big and peaches small, peaches white and peaches yellow, played a part in life from which they have somehow been deposed; every garden, almost every bush and the very boys' pockets grew them; they were "cut up" and eaten with cream at every meal; domestically "brandied" they figured, the rest of the year, scarce less freely—if they were rather a "party dish" it was because they made the party whenever they appeared, and when ice-cream was added, or they were added *to* it, they formed the highest revel we knew. Above all the public heaps of them, the high-piled receptacles at every turn, touched the street as with a sort of southern plenty. . . . We ate everything in those days by the bushel and the barrel, as from stores that were infinite.

The two passages illuminate clearly the workings of memory in one artist to the end of autobiography and the workings of memory in another artist to the subtler end of fiction. The common ground on which both stand is in their attempt to render the truth of experience. The Proustian food is not mere enumeration, mingled with a kind of smacking of the lips that one senses in the Jamesian memories; in each case each item matches the season, the occasion, the opportunity, and each season, occasion, and opportunity is the rationale of Françoise's choice; so that what has been evoked in the Proustian autobiography that is fiction, as distinct from the Jamesian autobiography that is autobiography, is also a subtle and studied characterization of Françoise—the brill, "because she had seen a beauty in the market," the roast mutton, "because the fresh air made one hungry and there would be plenty of time for it to 'settle down' in the seven hours before dinner," and so on.

What this can be held to demonstrate is that fiction can be autobiographical, but that this does not mean that it is autobiography. And while this may seem a truism, it must be stated so that we may attempt to determine the extent to which a work can be dissociated from the life that produces it.

2

Proceeding in this empirical fashion, let us now glance briefly at two works which have been fortuitously preserved. They were discarded by their authors who, in the very process of writing them, were making certain important discoveries about their art—and about themselves—discoveries indeed that prompted them to set aside these early attempts. They had outlived their usefulness even before completion. The first is the fragment, *Stephen Hero*, which consists of the materials Joyce finally worked into the last chapter of *A Portrait of the Artist as a Young Man*, but which is almost as long as the final novel. The second is the 300,000-word incomplete novel, *Jean Santeuil* (incomplete, though it is the equivalent of at least three modern-length novels). This was discovered among Proust's papers and was published in three volumes with a preface by André Maurois. Chance has thus provided us with a glimpse into two autobiographical novels, both in their primitive and almost wholly autobiographical state. This is a remarkable stroke of fortune for criticism. We are given an opportunity to see the artists making their false starts, recognizing their mistakes, and consciously rectifying them.

In both cases these—shall we call them preliminary?— works are remarkable, as they well might be, given the pens that wrote them. *Jean Santeuil*, which, for all its incompleteness, it is difficult to speak of as a fragment, stands as a beautifully written and very finely *felt* work that would have placed Proust high in the ranks of twentieth-century French writers even if he had written nothing else. *Stephen Hero*, this more truly a fragment, has much of the Joycean verbal magic even if it is without the virtuoso touches of the novelist's later writing. Both are derived from the daily lives of their authors. Joyce indeed spoke of the *Portrait* or *Stephen Hero* as his "autobiographical" novel in a letter to his publisher. Proust sought to conceal the autobiography behind an elaborate prologue quite in the manner of Henry James. He turned himself into a first-person narrator who listens to the novel *Jean Santeuil* as it is read aloud by a great novelist during their stay in a farmhouse in Brittany. A little preface of three sentences admits that the work is autobiographical, except that we are supposed to regard this as the preface of the novelist in the story, not of Proust the young listener and admirer:

> May I call this book a novel? It is less than a novel and perhaps much more, the very essence of my life, gathered with nothing added to it, in those hours of laceration in which it was lived. This book was never created; it was harvested. [*Ce livre n'a jamais été fait, il a été récolté.*]

And André Maurois, one of Proust's biographers and critics, confirms the fact that *Jean Santeuil* is very close to Proust's own life. In the novel's opening pages we discover the episode of the good-night kiss that will colour the launching of the mind's drama in *Swann's Way*; a childish episode with a girl named Marie forecasts the story of Gilberte. The Proust parents (still alive when this was written in the late 1890s) are drawn in greater detail, apparently from life. Bergotte is there, but as painter rather than writer. There is a direct presentation of the tumult of emotion aroused by the Dreyfus case that will be treated later in much more indirect fashion. The *petite phrase* is clearly from a work by Saint-Saëns. The theme of homosexuality appears, but faintly. The central portion of the book shows Jean in society and much of this is painted from the same palette as the later work. The lilacs bloom, perhaps with a less delicate odour. The book is the work of a Proust who has not yet discovered Ruskin. There is no Swann, and no Charlus, but—and this is extremely important—there are incidents in Jean's life which will later be incorporated into the life of Swann. At moments Proust is near his later search for involuntary memory, but it is not yet quite that; rather it is memory transposed into a direct and felt immediate reality. The haunting and poetic unity of the later work is here in an attenuated form. What we have is directness and freshness. We catch Proust in the process of his development and writing autobiography—the memoir in the form of a novel.

So in *Stephen Hero* certain of the fully developed scenes will later be treated in an indirect fashion or be dropped altogether. Joyce's first style is simple, matter-of-fact, frugal; and there is a bareness in the catalogue of Stephen's feelings and doings at the university which is in striking contrast to the work that emerged from it. The incident of Joyce's paper on "Drama and Life" and his proposal to Emma that she become his mistress, which stands out here as evidence of Stephen's juvenility, are later pushed aside. What we get largely is a picture of an aggressive young artist, suffering from a constant need to assert himself in his drab surroundings and in a life he finds stifling. He is defending himself against the world at every turn. This he does by a cold intellectualism, an eloquence that borders on constant speech-making, a search for the esoteric in scholarship and the assumption of an attitude defiant and arrogant.

In this fragment we are given Stephen's theory of art much as it was to be enunciated in *A Portrait of the Artist,* but it is here broken up among other episodes, and its exposition lacks the unity and coherence it will have later. In the successor work the statement on art marks Stephen's arrival at intellectual maturity. Once he has defined a theory of art, he is at the end of his youth. The artist as a young man may go out into the world and begin to fashion his work.

One element in the aesthetics of *Stephen Hero* is omitted from the *Portrait*. This is the theory of the epiphany. Joyce dropped this from the early draft, almost as if it were a private device, a personal matter. He alludes to it only later, in passing, in *Ulysses* and in terms that show he considered it as belonging to his nonage:

Remember your epiphanies on green oval leaves, deeply deep, copies to be sent if you died to all the great libraries of the world, including Alexandria?

Like *Jean Santeuil*, *Stephen Hero* has freshness and direct-ness, an acuteness of observation and sharpness of style which make us regret that more of it was not preserved when, so the story runs, Nora Joyce snatched it from the fire into which her husband had thrown it.

What the two artists did when they discarded these earlier works and started afresh was curiously similar. Proust rewrote *Jean Santeuil* into a first-person novel in which we are almost wholly in the narrator's mind. Hav-ing tried to be scrupulously objective (and having utilized the mechanism of a story within a story, and a narrator) he now candidly gave his novel an autobiographical cast. We may speculate that the death of his parents made the earlier reticences unnecessary; and the development of his process of self-examination through accretion of reverie and memory made the first person the only *truthful* way in which the self-examination could be reported without having to go through the technical difficulties involved in transferring this to another consciousness. Joyce, in both the early version and the final form of the *Portrait*, maintained the third person, but he turned a narrative wholly objective into one wholly subjective. In both cases the rewriting was in pursuit of subjective ex-perience: a need to look into the mind, inward that is, as well as outward from the mind at the world.

In a sense, therefore, these novels became more deeply autobiographical than before. Yet in another sense they were farther removed from autobiography, for, as we have seen, that which was Proust's biography now became part of the biography of Swann, even as the mind of Joyce, creating the mind of Stephen, in due course was to father Leopold and Molly Bloom. It is at this point, therefore, that we can profitably try to refine the question of the relationship between autobiography and the psychological novel.

3

In a broad sense, that is in a general psychological sense, everything we do is an expression of ourselves. How we walk and how we talk, the nervous impulses that drive our pen across a sheet and give an individual form to our handwriting, the words we speak and the phrases and sentences we build out of them, the images we conjure up and the objects our eyes select, these are all autobiographical acts, so that a book we write is the book of ourselves. When a poet writes the simplest lyric his choice of word and image and symbol is *his* and no one else's; and if he is guilty of plagiarism he has still made a choice in cribbing from one writer rather than from another. It is still a self-revealing act. In a world of multiple choices there is always a reason, although it may be obscure, why one choice is made rather than another. And it is on this ground that criticism, which seeks to discern the quality of the mind that produced a given work, has every reason to invoke the aid of the biographer. Indeed, the passion to discover the mind behind the work as well as the mind *in* the work explains why, failing to find the man Shakespeare, a whole school of speculation has discovered a compelling need to create another man. Perhaps all this is another way of saying that the style is the man. But it means also that the man is the style; that fragments of experience of the man have been moulded to produce the art, and that if we knew enough about any artist we could redissolve his art and find in it the biographical ingredients that shaped it. This would certainly be the case with the psychological novelist, even more than with the conventional novelist, since he gives us access to his mind.

The three main streams of consciousness in *Ulysses* spring from a single source; however different each may be, they are tributaries of the central stream of consciousness that feeds them. This central stream was the mind of James Joyce. The question which we must ask, therefore, is this: Is not a novel using stream-of-consciousness devices by its very nature an autobiographical novel? Does not such a novel tell us a great deal more than most novels about the mind of its writer? Are we not being given the very texture of the writer's experience and the very atmosphere of *his* mind? In a word, is not stream-of-consciousness writing another form of memoir-writing, that is a recapturing of the past of the writer, as if he had decided to write his memoirs? Is he not shuffling associations and memories in the pretence that they are fiction, or transferring them to characters (really disguises of himself) to create the impression that they belong to someone else? And if that be the case, what difference is there between memoirs such as Saint-Simon's and a novel of Proust's? Was not Casanova, in setting down his adventures, writing memoirs of his over-active life as fact, just as Proust was writing the memoirs of his over-active mind as fiction?

If we accept this line of argument, then we must agree that Marcel Proust wrote autobiography and not a novel, since he was forever reaching into his own mind and re-creating his own past in his search for the truths of experience. And yet Proust—who went so far as to call his hero Marcel—was the first to deny over and over again that he was writing autobiographical fiction. He was constantly asked about the persons he had put into his novel; and he constantly replied that he had created these persons himself.

"In this book," he writes in his last volume (in the magnificent summing up in which he examines himself as the artist who makes and preserves experience), "in this book in which there is not a single personage à clef, where I have invented everything to suit the requirements of my presentation . . ."

On first reading this we are tempted to proclaim it an audacious falsehood. Proust writes a novel that can stem only out of his own experience, he names his hero after himself, he tells his story in the first person, and he boldly proclaims—he has written a fiction! Nevertheless, as we pursue Proust's meaning we discover that he is stating a fundamental truth. "In writing," he says, ". . . there is not a single invented character to whom he [the author] could not give sixty names of people he has observed, of whom one poses for a grimace, another for an eye-glass, another for his temper, another for a particular movement of the arms." And he adds: "It is the feeling for the general in the potential writer which selects material suitable to a work of art because of its generality." So Henry James pleaded with his brother, his aunt, his close friends, who told him he had cruelly caricatured Miss Peabody of Boston, Hawthorne's sister-in-law, in his portrait of the social reformer in *The Bostonians*. James replied that the character was evolved "entirely from my moral consciousness, like every other person I have ever drawn." She was perhaps a synthesis of several Boston women, and we have no reason to doubt the truth of James's assertion. Yet it is interesting to reflect that between the name of the Peabody of life and the Miss Birdseye of James's fiction there is a strange resemblance. Is not a bird's eye virtually a pea-body? Unconsciously James, seeking a type, may have reproduced an observed character. Both novelists would agree, however, that in the process, within the "moral consciousness," the character was re-created.

Characters in fiction are composites, as most novelists tell us. So too the characters in Proust acquire bits of their biography from Proust himself and from the observed details which his detail-searching mind treasured. But it is interesting to discover that even the celebrated *petite phrase*, that haunting *moment musical* which weaves its way through the *Temps Perdu*, is a composite phrase; for in a letter to Jacques de Lacretelle Proust describes it as an "infinitely mediocre phrase of a Saint-Saëns violin sonata, a musician I don't like" (and so it appeared in *Jean Santeuil*), yet later it is the "Good Friday spell," and when the piano and violin sound like two birds it is the César Franck sonata as played by Georges Enesco; the tremolo reminds him of the prelude to *Lohengrin*, but it is also a prelude by Schubert and a piece by Fauré. This use of the composite in Proustian creation will ultimately take another form in the work of Joyce; for there we shall find composites of language addressed to the evoking of composite associations.

We see, therefore, that while on the surface in Proust we may speak of the work as autobiography, what he is revealing to us is the complexity of his subject, himself as a complex being and the complexity of the people he knew: that we are all in a sense composites of parents and relations and memories, pastiches of the flesh, resembling now one person and now another; that man is not one but many, and we thus obtain from Proust a sense of the variousness and the depth of experience. In the technical sense Proust is writing autobiographical fiction; in the larger sense he has created a synthesis that is art independent of its creator. In the same way I would say that in *Ulysses*, Joyce's three distinct streams of consciousness, though tributaries of his own stream, stand as independent personalities and not as different facets of James Joyce's personality, even though we might, by close searching, say that Molly Bloom expresses a certain part of the feminine in his nature as well as his experience of women and is perhaps a synthesis of all the women he has known, while Bloom has those obsessive qualities which Joyce himself had and revealed in carrying through a work such as *Finnegans Wake*.

For all this, we find in Proust sometimes a deliberate and curious blurring of the dividing line between autobiography and fiction. In Swann he creates a character distinct from the narrator Marcel, in the same sense that Bloom possesses his own striking identity for all that he is a projection of Joyce. In the first part of the *Temps Perdu*, Proust introduces what amounts to a separate *nouvelle*, the story of "Swann in Love", which stands out as an almost conventional piece of fiction tied by many visible and invisible threads to the rest of the work. As Proust sets out to tell this story he seems inclined to divorce the narrative from the mind of his narrator. But he cannot bring himself to do so. His intellectual probity tells him that a connecting link remains. And so he analyses what this process involves.

Swann's affair with Odette, he tells us, had occurred before Marcel was born. Proust, therefore, can only be, so to speak, Swann's biographer. The story was told him, he says, "with that accuracy of detail which it is easier, often, to obtain when we are studying the lives of people who have been dead for centuries than when we are trying to chronicle those of our own most intimate friends." Nevertheless, he will not write biography. He draws the story into himself and turns it into part of Marcel's story. For the stories he heard about Swann were condensed, he says, "into a single substance" in his mind, "but had not so far coalesced that I could not discern between the three strata, between my oldest, my instinctive memories, those others, inspired more recently by a taste or 'perfume' and those which were actually the memories of another, from whom I had acquired them at second hand—no fissures, indeed, no geological faults, but at least those veins, those streaks of colour which in certain rocks, in certain marbles, point to differences of origin, age and formation."

This geological analogy, evolved for the grouping of his different memories, is strangely like William James's picture of memory in which he says the "transition between the thought of one object and the thought of another is no more a break in the *thought* than a joint in a bamboo is a break in the wood. It is a part of the *consciousness* as much as the joint is a part of the bamboo." So Swann and the story of his misadventure in love have become a part of the consciousness of Marcel; and Swann, unlike Bloom, is not projected as separate from Marcel's mind; he remains a layer of memory in the strata of Marcel's mind. But he has a separate identity within that memory.

Memory in Proust, therefore, is not the mere act of recalling events in a given sequence, ordinarily chronological, which is what we usually think of as being autobiography. Proust tries to show us that memory is composite, a process of free association which shuffles events out of sequence like a pack of cards and across great gaps of time, so that we continue to see people as young who have grown old, and to think of people alive who are dead, and recover places and scenes that have changed or vanished altogether. Proust said that "memory, by introducing the past into the present without modification, as though it were the present, eliminates precisely that great Time-dimension in accordance with which life is realised." And this, by its very nature, becomes a synthetic process.

A work of art is thus not just a sum of its parts, that is a sum of things remembered by the artist. A great soldier will set down his memories, in sequence, of battles fought, adventures lived, honours won and personalities encountered, and they might make interesting reading, like the sequences of events that fill a daily newspaper. But we do not consider this art. Certainly we can consider it autobiography. These same memories, fused into a synthesis of experience, blended with the texture of life, as the battles are in *War and Peace* or in the historical panorama of *La Chartreuse de Parme*, become a work of art: it is the way the disparate elements have been fused and brought together, the raw materials transformed by the illumination of the mind into the work that, beyond its temporal significance, becomes a part of the experience of successive generations of readers.

4

What view did Joyce have of this problem of the artist's relation to his material, he who was so articulate and logical in the creation of his personal aesthetic? He has offered us a very cogent statement embodied toward the end of *A Portrait of the Artist as a Young Man*. I have already used portions of this passage to illustrate specific points, but now I would like to quote the entire statement:

The lyrical form is in fact the simplest verbal vesture of an instant of emotion, a rhythmical cry such as ages ago cheered on the man who pulled at the oar or dragged stones up a slope. He who utters it is more conscious of the instant of emotion than of himself as feeling emotion. The simplest epical form is seen emerging out of lyrical literature when the artist prolongs and broods upon himself as the centre of an epical event and this form progresses till the centre of emotional gravity is equidistant from the artist himself and from others. The narrative is no longer purely personal. The personality of the artist passes into the narration itself, flowing round and round the persons and the action like a vital sea. This progress you will see easily in that old English ballad *Turpin Hero* which begins in the first person and ends in the third person. The dramatic form is reached when the vitality which has flowed and eddied round each person fills every person with such vital force that he or she assumes a proper and intangible esthetic life. The personality of the artist, at first a cry or a cadence or a mood and then a fluid and lambent narrative, finally refines itself out of existence, impersonalises itself, so to speak. The esthetic image in the dramatic form is life purified in and reprojected from the human imagination. The mystery of esthetic, like that of material creation, is accomplished. The artist, like the God of creation, remains within or behind or beyond or above his handiwork, invisible, refined out of existence, indifferent, paring his fingernails.

Like Proust, then, Joyce reaches the conclusion that although fictional characters begin in the first person they can end in the third, having taken their vitality from their creator; the creator, theoretically at least, removes himself into the anonymity of a seemingly disinterested spectator. The picture Joyce dresses before us of lyric-epic-dramatic is not unlike the picture he evoked in the Holles Street lying-in hospital where Stephen waits with the medical students for the birth of the child; this episode is told in a parody of English literature proceeding from the infant gurglings of the baby (lyrical), to the sophisticated prose of the nineteenth century. In essence what Joyce is describing, in defining the evolution of the drama from the lyric cry by transition through the epic, is not unlike the picture Freud drew of the stages of man's development, again from the infant cry, lyrical, for milk, to be followed by the growing awareness that milk appeases hunger, and then a further awareness that the breast or bottle which supplies the milk is related to other persons, leading to awareness of self in relation to an object or person, which is the general stage at which the infant takes the path of his ultimate adulthood. The artist goes beyond such awareness. He is aware not only of his relationship to the object or person, but *of the awareness of others in their relationship to the object*. When the artist gives a dramatic picture of these relationships and the feelings that are involved in them, he has successfully removed himself within, behind, above, or beyond his creation.

I think, however, that Joyce is not quite right in saying that the artist has been, by this process, refined out of existence. The dissociation is not complete. He remains, after all, within, behind, above, or beyond the work—and not too far beyond. He is like those dreams we have in which we are both the actor and the audience; in which we act and also stand by watching ourselves in action. So a work of fiction, if not autobiography of the artist, is still a particular synthesis created by him, and by no one else. We can thus push our inquiry a step farther, to what seems to me the inevitable conclusion: that there remains a quality of mind that informs a work, no matter how much the artist has disengaged himself. This cannot be refined away. When James gives us his experience of looking at posters as a boy, the characteristic personality of James is there, even as we have Proust's when the little Proust boy studies his posters. When the kind lady of legend handed a certain little musical theme to Brahms and to Grieg it became a Brahms rhapsody in one case and the music of Asa's death in Grieg's *Peer Gynt* suite in the other. In both cases the theme was the same; and yet the Brahms rhapsody would never be taken for a work by Grieg, nor the Grieg work be considered as written by Brahms. What is the whole history of the novel if not a history of minds, like Balzac's or Flaubert's, Stendhal's or Tolstoy's, Dickens's or James's, Proust's or Joyce's? We are always aware of these minds and their vision which plays from page to page, although what they have created is fiction.

Henry James, in his essay on "The Art of Fiction," has admirably expressed this, while at the same time showing how observation, added to a rich experience, can perform the synthesis that we call art:

I remember an English novelist [he writes], a woman of genius, telling me that she was much commended for the impression she had managed to give in one of her tales of the nature and way of life of the French Protestant youth. She had been asked where she learned so much about this recondite being, she had been congratulated on her peculiar opportunities. These opportunities consisted in her having once, in Paris, as she ascended a staircase, passed an open door where, in the household of a *pasteur*, some of the young Protestants were seated at table round a finished meal. The glimpse made a picture; it lasted only a moment, but that moment was experience. She had got her direct personal impression, and she turned out her type. She knew what youth was, and what Protestantism; she also had the advantage of having seen what it was to be French, so that she converted these ideas into a concrete image and produced a reality. . . . The power to guess the unseen from the seen, to trace the implication of things, to judge the whole piece by the pattern, the condition of feeling life in general so completely that you are well on your way to knowing any particular corner of it—this cluster of gifts may almost be said to constitute experience.

This power to "have the implication of things" and to "guess the unseen from the seen" is what Proust was alluding to when he spoke of the way in which his characters and incidents were composites of experience. Beside the Jamesian passage it is useful to place Browning's discussion of the "subjective" poet in his essay on Shelley, in which he probes the relation between the work of art produced and the mind in which it was fashioned:

Not with the combination of humanity in action, but with the primal elements of humanity he has to do; and he digs where he stands,—preferring to seek them in his own soul as the nearest reflex of that absolute Mind, according to the intuitions of which he desires to perceive and speak. Such a poet does not deal habitually with the picturesque groupings and tempestuous tossings of the forest-trees, but with their roots and fibres naked to the chalk and stone. He does not paint pictures and hang them on the walls, but rather carries them on the retina of his own eyes: we must look deep into his human eyes, to see those pictures on them. He is rather a seer, accordingly, than a fashioner, and what he produces will be less a work than an effluence. That effluence cannot be easily considered in abstraction from his personality,—being indeed the very radiance and aroma of his personality, projected from it but not separated ... readers of his poetry must be readers of his biography also.

What Browning said of the subjective poet can be applied to the subjective novelist; and if, instead of the word "biography," we read "quality of mind"—for this in essence is what he means—we arrive at a vision of the creative process analogous to that of James, Proust, and Joyce.

Of the psychological novelists, James Joyce perhaps more than Proust, in *Ulysses* and in *Finnegans Wake*, removed himself farthest from his work. Proust and Dorothy Richardson, much less, inevitably, because of the very way in which they sought to capture subjective experience, through a single consciousness. Proust recognized this when he said that "the great men of letters have never created more than a single work, or rather have never done more than refract through various mediums an identical beauty which they bring into the world." This is not in contradiction to what he also said about his work as fiction. He was recognizing the peculiar quality of mind that pervades each work of literary art, the quality by which we recognize it as the work of that mind and of no other. And this is so even when we have no biography of the creating mind—as in the case of Shakespeare, whom we do not know save as the most shadowy of shadows, but whose mind remains richly present among us. Or even Homer, who is more shadowy still.

CHAPTER X

THE NOVEL AS POEM

THROUGHOUT OUR inquiry into the psychological novel we have been confronted by a paradox. We have observed that the novelists begin as naturalists or realists —and end as symbolists! In their pursuit of shadowy, dancing, flowing thought they invoke prose—and produce poetry! What begins as an attempt to click the mind's shutter and catch the images of outer reality impinging upon it, ends as an impressionist painting. Perhaps this proves that the dividing line between the artist who wants to use prose to paint his picture and the artist to whom experience can be rendered only as poetry is indeed narrow. Perhaps it proves that the symbolists were the greater realists in recognizing that literature must recreate life, not attempt merely to document it.

The reason for our paradox is not hard to find. The stream-of-consciousness novel approaches the condition of poetry because the writer holds in his hand one medium only with which to create his work. He has words, even as the painter has colour and the musician sound. The novelist sets out to use words to render the very iridescence and bloom of life or to frame in syllables the light and the dark moments of memory and feeling. The "word" must paint a picture, or convey the sound of a freight train rushing through the night and through the mind of Molly Bloom; it must remind the reader of a smell or a lost sensation. And it must be so used by the writer as to convey to the reader at least some of the feelings the writer experienced at the moment he used it. The word is asked to carry, on shoulders not broad enough, the whole of a writer's experience.

But words, for all their richness and malleability, are curiously rigid. Each word acquires a history, a long history, as the semanticists tell us, and not only a history etymological but a history emotional as well. Words are our language of communication, and while we convey general meanings to each other in using them, each word also acquires a special meaning, for both the user and the listener. To the literary artist seeking to catch the atmosphere of the mind, words are a stock-in-trade as difficult to handle as paints are to a painter who would try to depict sound on canvas. A painter may paint a picture of a train rushing through the night in such a way that those of us looking at the picture will, with our inner ear, hear its rushing sound, even though the canvas remains motionless. So the user of words may find syllables to suggest colour which only our inner eye will perceive:

Going and coming, beckoning, signalling, so the light and shadow, which now made the wall grey, now the bananas bright yellow, now made the Strand grey, now made the omnibuses bright yellow, seemed to Septimus Warren Smith lying on the sofa in the sitting-room; watching the watery gold glow and fade with the astonishing sensibility of some live creature on the roses, on the wall-paper.

Virginia Woolf here asks the reader to imagine a grey wall and a grey Strand, yellow bananas and yellow omnibuses, watery gold glow and roses on wall-paper. Yet even here, with the invoking of exact words representing colours, some readers will imagine primary colours and some will experience different shadings, for the yellow of bananas is not necessarily the yellow of an omnibus, and the roses on the wall-paper are all the colours of roses—indeed most of us would imagine those roses as red, but some person might think of them as yellow too. What happens to the stream-of-consciousness writer, in using words in this fashion to record emotion and fleeting impression, is inevitable and clearly predictable. We can see it happening in the later novels of Henry James as he pushes more deeply into the minds and feelings of his characters—and *he* is not writing stream of consciousness but catching only the mood or tone of contemplation and reverie. He begins to use vivid metaphor increasingly; as he proceeds the metaphors become elaborate in the extreme, image piled upon image, into vast superstructures. The confirmed artist in prose finds himself functioning as a poet.

This situation had been occupying, for months and months, the very centre of the garden of her life, but it had reared itself there like some strange, tall tower of ivory, or perhaps rather some wonderful, beautiful, but outlandish pagoda, a structure plated with hard, bright porcelain, coloured and figured and adorned, at the over-hanging eaves, with silver bells that tinkled, ever so charmingly, when stirred by chance airs. She had walked round and round it—that was what she felt. . . . The great decorated surface had remained consistently impenetrable and inscrutable.

Or the imagery of the following passage:

The suggestion as of a creature consciously floating and shining in a warm summer sea, some element of dazzling sapphire and silver, a creature cradled upon depths, buoyant among dangers, in which fear or folly, or sinking otherwise than in play, was impossible. . . . The beauty of her condition was keeping him, at any rate, as he might feel, in sight of the sea, where, though his personal dips were over, the whole thing could shine at him, and the air and the plash and the play become for him too a sensation.

The writer attempting to create the illusion of a mind flowing with thought and image and impression turns to the symbolist poet; he calls upon all the devices of prosody, exploiting the resources of the language in the belief that it is the writer's task to make the word fit the thought, to match the language of the mind, and if necessary to invent a language that will render it :

Look, look, the dusk is growing! My branches lofty are taking root. And my cold cher's gone ashley. Fieluhr? Filou! What age is at? It saon is late. 'Tis endless now senne eye or erewone last saw Waterhouse's clogh. They took it asunder, I hurd thum sigh. When will they reassemble it? O, my back, my back, my bach! I'd want to go to Aches-les-Pains. Pingpong! There's the Belle for Sexaloitez! And Concepta de Send-us-pray! Pang! Wring out the clothes! Wring in the dew! Godavari, vert the showers! And grant thaya grace!

Aman. Will we spread them here now? Ay, we will. Flip!
Spread on your bank and I'll spread mine on mine. Flep!
It's what I'm doing. Spread!

Or again

Teems of times and happy returns. The seim anew. Ordo-
vico or viricordo. Anna was, Livia is, Plurabelle's to be. North-
men's thing made southfolk's place, but howmulty plurators
made eachone in person? Latin me that, my trinity scholard,
out of eure sanscreed into oure eryan. *Hircus Civis Eblanensis*!
He had buckgoat paps on him, soft ones for orphans. Ho, Lord!
Twins of his bosom. Lord save us! And ho! Hey? What all
men. Hot? His tittering daughters of. Whawk?

Howmulty plurators made eachone in person? Howmulty indeed. That sense of plurality and of the multitudinous in
things which Joyce experienced was the logical, the inevitable, the inexorable end-point of the attempt to make
language describe and evoke the texture of the mind. Beyond a given point inner reality dissolves into what we
have spoken of as halos, fringes, auras of experience, that
can no longer be rendered as continuous narrative, nor
have the sequence, coherence, or order which the novelist
of the past tried to give to the novel. What prevails instead is the condition of poetry in which we catch what
Browning spoke of as the "effluence" of the artist's mind.
In a different context Wordsworth saw poetry as a
remembrance of things past, "the spontaneous overflow
of powerful feeling . . . recollected in tranquillity" and
Coleridge saw fancy as "memory emancipated from the
order of time and space." "In truth," wrote Proust, "the
events of a life present no interest when they are shorn of
all the feeling which makes of them a poem" and he said
also: "As art exactly recomposes life, an atmosphere of
poetry surrounds those truths within ourselves, to which
we attain." And again, Proust said: "Metaphor alone can
give a sort of eternity to style." He complained that there
wasn't a single fine metaphor in the whole of Flaubert!

2

Virginia Woolf was not one of the architects of the
stream-of-consciousness novel. She read Joyce, Proust,

and Dorothy Richardson and absorbed their lesson. Her peculiar contribution to the novel of subjectivity lay in her awareness almost from the first that she could obtain given effects of experience by a constant search for the condition of poetry. The influence of James Joyce upon her is much more profound than is generally believed. Indeed, she herself was prompt to seize upon *Ulysses* as a transcendent work long before it was published and only a few chapters had been serialized. She wrote at the time:

> Anyone who had read the *Portrait of the Artist as a Young Man* or, what promises to be a far more interesting work, *Ulysses,* now appearing in the *Little Review*, will have hazarded some theory . . . as to Mr. Joyce's intention. On our part, with such a fragment before us, it is hazarded rather than affirmed; but whatever the intention of the whole, there can be no question but that it is of the utmost sincerity and that the result, difficult or unpleasant as we may judge it, is undeniably important. . . . Mr. Joyce . . . is concerned at all costs to reveal the flickerings of that innermost flame which flashes its messages through the brain, and in order to preserve it he disregards with complete courage whatever seems to him adventitious, whether it be probability, or coherence, or any other of those signposts which for generations have served to support the imagination of a reader when called upon to imagine what he can neither touch nor see. . . . If we want life itself, here surely we have it.

She was to have reservations about Joyce, but these were to be, in effect, afterthoughts. The impression he made on her was powerful. Her first two novels, *The Voyage Out* and *Night and Day*, published in 1915 and 1919, were conventional enough. The narrative proceeded in a traditional progression and there was no attempt to go very far into the minds of the characters. There are, however, interesting portents of what was to come (as there are in the short stories in which she was experimenting). In *The Voyage Out* one of the characters observes: "What I want to do in writing novels is very much what you want to do when you play the piano, I expect. We want to find out what's behind things, don't we?—Look at the lights down there scattered about anyhow. Things I feel come to me like lights. . . . I want to combine them. . . . Have you ever seen fireworks that make figures? . . . I want to make figures."

In this novel a woman looks at a circular, iridescent patch in the river, watching it with fascination and weaving thoughts around it. The patch is like the distant series of lights; it is the pin-point of experience, the grains of sand, the mark on the wall around which Virginia Woolf will have the mind accumulate its associations. Her method seems to be a focusing of the mind in this fashion, in the way in which animals and people—and notably in certain types of mental ailments—will look at some pinpoint with a fascination all-absorbing, unable to tear themselves away from it. Such a focusing occurs in the works of Mrs Woolf, and around this she gives us the cluster of emotion and memory. By this process she achieves a remarkable, shimmering effect of experience. Light, tone, colour play through her cadenced works in a constant search for mood and with no attempt to impart an individual character to the style of thought. There is no attempt at portrait painting; rather does she try to evoke a state of feeling by a kind of mental poesy. The same vein of poetry runs through all the minds she creates for us. It is as if she had created a single device or convention, to be applied universally, in the knowledge that the delicacy of her perception, the waves of feeling, will wash over her readers as she washes them over her characters.

This is alike her achievement and its fatal flaw. The bright flame-like vividness of her books creates beautiful illuminated surfaces. There is no tragic depth in them, only the pathos of things lost and outlived, the past irretrievable or retrieved as an ache in the present. And in this she has fused the example of Proust as of Joyce. I think of *Mrs Dalloway* as a Joycean novel, diluted, and washed and done in beautiful water-colour; and *To the Lighthouse* is Proustian in its time-sense, but again the medium is a kind of water-colour of the emotions.

Like Proust and Joyce, Virginia Woolf clearly expressed her aesthetic of fiction. Once she had grasped the lesson of her two great predecessors, she seems to have known exactly how she would apply it. But her definition of fiction is more impressionistic than the carefully evolved analysis Proust made of his *métier*, or the Aquinian aesthetic of Joyce. She adds little to what has been said, and once we divest her ideas of the eloquence in which they are clothed, we find them rather thin and unoriginal. Precisely because it has become one of her most quoted passages, I want to repeat here Virginia Woolf's account of what she believed should be the material of the novel of subjectivity:

Examine for a moment an ordinary mind on an ordinary day. The mind receives a myriad impressions—trivial, fantastic, evanescent, or engraved with the sharpness of steel. From all sides they come, an incessant shower of innumerable atoms; and as they fall, as they shape themselves into the life of Monday or Tuesday, the accent falls differently from of old; the moment of importance came not here but there; so that if a writer were a free man and not a slave, if he could write what he chose, not what he must, if he could base his work upon his own feeling and not upon convention, there would be no plot, no comedy, no tragedy, no love interest or catastrophe in the accepted style, and perhaps not a single button sewn on as the Bond Street tailors would have it. Life is not a series of gig lamps symmetrically arranged but a luminous halo, a semi-transparent envelope surrounding us from the beginning of consciousness to the end. Is it not the task of the novelist to convey this varying, this unknown and uncircumscribed spirit, whatever aberration or complexity it may display, with as little mixture of the alien and external as possible? We are not pleading merely for courage and sincerity; we are suggesting that the proper stuff of fiction is a little other than custom would have us believe it.

This is very beautifully stated, but I am tempted to suggest that Benjamin Constant expressed it much more succinctly long before. I translate freely:

Man's feelings are mixed and confused; they are composed of a multitude of varied impressions which escape observation; and words, always clumsy and too general, may well serve to designate but never to define them.

Virginia Woolf tried to catch the shower of innumerable atoms, the vision of life, the iridescence, the luminous halo. It was her way of circumventing the clumsiness of words. She went on to specify:

> Let us record the atoms as they fall upon the mind in the order in which they fall, let us trace the pattern, however disconnected and incoherent in appearance, which each sight or incident scores upon that consciousness. . . . Any method is right, every method is right, that expresses what we wish to express, if we are writers; that brings us closer to the novelist's intention, if we are readers . . . everything is the proper stuff of fiction, every feeling, every thought, every quality of brain and spirit is drawn upon; no perception comes amiss.

This, however, comes much more closely to describing the writing of Dorothy Richardson than the art of Virginia Woolf. However much Mrs Woolf might assert the need to record the shower of atoms "in the order in which they fall," she neither accepted that order, nor believed in describing their frequent incoherence. Her method was that of the lyric poet. She was interested in the sharpened image, the moment, the condensed experience. She saw the world around her as if it were a sharp knife cutting its way into her being.

From James Joyce, Virginia Woolf seems to have obtained a certain sense of *oneness* and the isolation that resides within it: from him she learned how to give meaning to the simultaneity of experience. London is to Mrs Dalloway what Dublin is to Leopold Bloom. But her London is a large canvas background with light cleverly playing over it and, unlike Joyce, her people are distillations of mind and flesh. Clarissa Dalloway's day in London, also a day in June, as in *Ulysses*, begins at nine in the morning and finishes early the next morning. (Indeed, in most of Mrs Woolf's fiction, time is reduced to a few hours, so that even in *To the Lighthouse*, where a number of years are bridged in the middle passage, "Time Passes," it is but to link two single days at each end of that period.) Clarissa Dalloway walks through London, and the people around her form an encircling wave as she goes to Bond Street or strolls along the Green Park, while in the midst of the day the big bronze accents of Big Ben remind us of the ticking of mechanical time as we move in and out of Mrs

Dalloway's mind and the minds of the other characters in the story.

The book's structure seems largely to be modelled on the multiple-scened chapter in *Ulysses* which is tied together by the progress of the vice-regal cavalcade through Dublin's streets. We are in many minds in the streets of London. But Mrs Dalloway's mind, and that of Septimus Warren Smith, hold the centre of the book as did those of Bloom and Dedalus in *Ulysses*. The entire inwardness of the book, its limited time-scheme, the use of multiple views, so that we feel we have seen London through many eyes—and so are aware of it through many awarenesses—the glimpsing of certain characters and then the glimpse of them anew through the perceptions of the principal characters—all this becomes a subtle conversion to simpler ends of the Joycean complexities. But if Bloom and Dedalus are a father and son who meet for a brief moment at the end of a long day symbolically, as Odysseus met Telemachus after a lifetime of wanderings, Clarissa Dalloway and Septimus Smith seem to be two facets of the same personality—indeed, the projection by Virginia Woolf of two sides of herself. Mrs Woolf's diary shows that she conceived this novel as an attempt to show "the world seen by the sane and the insane side by side." And we know from her own preface to it that she first intended Septimus to have no existence: it was Clarissa who was to die or to kill herself at the end of her London day and her brilliant party. Finally, she envisaged Septimus as a "double" of Clarissa.

But how is he the double—Septimus the insane, Clarissa the sane? What connections, we might ask, unify them? They never actually meet, as Bloom and Dedalus did, although their paths converge during the day; and it is the doctor of Septimus, the clumsy inept Harley Street psychiatrist, who brings to Clarissa's party the little bit of news that Septimus has committed suicide. The imparting of this bit of information, a mere incident in a big city, remote from Clarissa, plunges her nevertheless into a deep fantasy and identification with the unknown man who is now dead.

What business had the Bradshaws to talk of death at her party? A young man had killed himself. And they talked of it at her party—the Bradshaws talked of death.

So far it is the intrusion of unpleasant reality, and Clarissa is hard at work trying to submerge her feelings. Then comes identification:

He had killed himself—but how? Always her body went through it first, when she was told, suddenly, of an accident; her dress flamed, her body burnt. He had thrown himself from a window. Up had flashed the ground; through him, blundering, bruising, went the rusty spikes. There he lay with a thud, thud, thud in his brain, and then a suffocation of blackness. So she saw it. But why had he done it? And the Bradshaws talked of it at her party!

This is Clarissa whom Peter had described as the "perfect hostess" and whom he had remembered as a girl, "timid, hard; something arrogant; unimaginative; prudish." There was a "coldness," a "woodenness," an "impenetrability" in her. But we know better; we know also that this façade of the perfect hostess submerges the Clarissa who has intuitions and feelings which she can never fully face. It is on the ground of the failure to feel that Clarissa and Septimus are each other's double. Septimus had choked feeling when his friend Evans was killed at his side during the war. He goes through life utterly numbed by this experience.

He could reason; he could read, Dante, for example, quite easily . . . he could add up his bill; his brain was perfect; it must be the fault of the world then—that he could not feel.

And so these two principal characters dissociate experience constantly from themselves. Both are incapable of establishing a meaningful relationship with the emotional texture of life: Clarissa escapes by giving some slight play to her insights and intuitions, "If you put her in a room with someone, up went her back like a cat's; or she purred," but the façade of the perfect hostess is untouched, the feeling submerged. Septimus escapes by throttling feeling and creating a new world within, filled with private

132

demons and private terrors, from which he can only seek, in the end, the swift obliteration of consciousness.

The whole of the novel conveys poignantly Virginia Woolf's response to Joyce's success in reflecting how, in a big city, people's paths cross and dramas go on within range of dramas, and yet in spite of innumerable points of superficial contact and relation, each drama is isolated and each individual remains locked within walls of private experience. The book's brilliance, as writing and as poetry, lies in the skill with which Mrs Woolf weaves from one mind into another. Septimus, in the park, sees a man walking towards him and suddenly invests him with the aspect of another man and the trauma of his war experience; and suddenly we are in the mind of the other man, Peter, who sees only a rather disturbed-looking Septimus and his anxious wife Rezia, without beginning to know what violent images have been flickering in Septimus's consciousness. This complex inner material could be rendered only by the use of brilliantly evocative prose-poetry. And this novel, like those which Virginia Woolf wrote after it, illustrates admirably the worth of the symbolist method in fiction. We have only to think of a Zola or a George Moore creating Clarissa after the manner of their naturalist doctrines to understand the difference. Clarissa would emerge as a commonplace woman, the façade described in detail, but no hint of the fascinating and troubled and mysterious personality behind her exterior. Mrs Woolf extended with remarkable skill and literary virtuosity the creation of a novel that conveys inner experience. She was capable of finding the words that would show the world through her protagonists' minds: and she participated fully in the significant shift of emphasis, inaugurated by Henry James, from the outer social world—as explored by Balzac or the naturalists—to the sensibility with which that outer world is appreciated and felt.

If the general plan, the painting of the environment, is a scaling down of Joycean architectonics, the painting of the sensibility tends to be Proustian. And yet there is a significant difference. In Proust the odour of the lilacs is directly felt and explored with subtlety; his feelings well up out of the page and are carefully communicated. In Mrs Woolf the odour bounces off the flowers and reaches the reader as a sharp, distinct but refracted sensation. One has indeed an effect of the bouncing-off of light and sound throughout the novel from people and objects and against the receiving mind. Proust touches experience directly. Mrs Woolf's method is refraction, through a kind of high, tense awareness. The poetry is there on every page and always a synthesis—a pulling together of objects and impressions. In addition to Big Ben heard by London and the people immediately around or near Mrs Dalloway, they watch an aeroplane sky-writing. The aeroplane serves to unify the city and the people as the vice-regal cavalcade did in *Ulysses*:

Ah, but that aeroplane! Hadn't Mrs. Dempster always longed to see foreign parts? She had a nephew, a missionary. It soared and shot. She always went on the sea at Margate, not out o' sight of land, but she had no patience with women who were afraid of water. It swept and fell. Her stomach was in her mouth. Up again. There's a fine young fellow aboard of it, Mrs. Dempster wagered, and away and away it went, fast and fading, away and away the aeroplane shot; soaring over Greenwich and all the masts; over the little island of grey churches, St. Paul's and the rest, till, on either side of London, fields spread out and dark brown woods where adventurous thrushes, hopping boldly, glancing quickly, snatched the snail and tapped him on a stone, once, twice, thrice.

This is stream-of-consciousness writing after the manner of Joyce and a fascinating dissociation of experience which Mrs Woolf always conveys to us, a matching of incongruities. From the broad skies we are swept across a vast city—and fixed on a pin-point. The world is blotted out; the eye leaves the plane to catch a predatory thrush bouncing a snail on a rock. The world can be reduced to a snail—but a snail can also become a pin-point of experience from which the mind moves out into the world. In *The Mark on the Wall* Virginia Woolf seeks to explain involuntary association and always with a sense that memory is an invoking of the incongruous. She sees a mark on the

wall. It seems to jut out. It is not entirely circular. It
seems to cast a shadow. Then:

> If I ran my finger down that strip of the wall it would, at a
> certain point, mount and descend a small tumulus, a smooth
> tumulus like those barrows on the South Downs, which are, they
> say, either tombs or camps. Of the two I should prefer them to
> be tombs, desiring melancholy like most English people . . .

and so on, a mark on the wall, a barrow, a tomb, and her
daydream continues to take wing like the aeroplane in the
sky over trees, rivers, the Downs, *Whitaker's Almanack*,
fields of asphodel, until someone standing beside her
brings her back to the reality, the room, the newspaper,
the mark on the wall, by saying: "All the same, I don't
see why we should have a snail on our wall."

3

Virginia Woolf's fiction took its sharp turn immediately
after the publication of *Ulysses*. After her first attempt at
stream-of-consciousness writing in *Jacob's Room* of 1922
and *Mrs Dalloway* of 1925 she wrote an essay that sought
to define her purpose. It appeared in 1927 in the *New
York Herald Tribune* book section. In it she argued that
the future of the novel inevitably had to be poetic; and
that the fiction-to-come would be written, one gathered,
in the way in which Virginia Woolf was writing her
novels. The prose would have many of the characteristics
of poetry. Poetry had failed to serve the twentieth century as it had the preceding centuries. The poetic novel
represented a compromise. "Prose has taken all the dirty
work on her own shoulders," Mrs Woolf wrote, "has
answered letters, paid bills, written articles, made
speeches, served the needs of business men, shopkeepers,
lawyers, soldiers." The compromise, Mrs Woolf pre-
dicted, would be the taking on by fiction of "something
of the exaltation of poetry, but much of the ordinariness
of prose."

This was written in 1927 before a great poetic novel,
perhaps the greatest, was published; indeed, it was then
only getting well under way, and I doubt whether

Virginia Woolf had such a work in mind. For that work, *Finnegans Wake*, seems to me to represent the final stage, the terminal point of the novel of subjectivity. After it there seems to be only a retracing of steps, a return to earlier forms, a reworking and perhaps intensification of earlier material. Joyce created it syllable by syllable, a great mass of sound, a long symphonic work. The written words of *Finnegans Wake* tease the intellectual part of our minds by their composite character and their elaborate many-languaged puns. But when we listen to the fragment Joyce recorded we discover the extent to which this book was written with the ear and for the ear even more than for the eye. The eye often stumbles over words that have a haunting beauty when they are read aloud:

Wait till the honeying of the lune, love! Die eve, little eve die! We see that wonder in your eye. We'll meet again, we'll part once more. The spot I'll seek if the hour you'll find. My chart shines high where the blue milk's upset. Forgivemequick, I'm going! Bubye! And you, pluck your watch, forgetmenot. Your evenlode. So save to jurna's end! My sights are swimming thicker on me by the shadows to this place. I sow home slowly now by own way, moyvalley way. Towy I too, rathmine.

In *Finnegans Wake* Joyce no longer attempts to give us consciousness but gropes toward that discovery of the condition of sleep that Proust essayed, and toward the rendering of the unconscious. Man is no longer an individual, we feel him in the mass, Here Comes Everybody. The book is a vast symphonic verbal synthesis, an attempt to render the collective mind and the collective unconscious.

CHAPTER XI

THE IMAGE IN THE MIRROR

IN ESSENCE ours has been an inquiry into the capacity of language to record inner experience, and the capacity of the novel form to convey it. We have seen how within the novel, once there is inclusion of large masses of subjective matter, there is an alteration of the temporal and indeed spatial qualities of the fiction. Mechanical time gives way to psychological time; thought is shown in its flowing kinetic state; but the process of recording it results, in reality, in a kind of stasis, so that the inner monologue or stream can be said to be *observed* as well as overheard. And the observation is immediate. Since thought does not arrange itself in orderly sequence, the novel of subjectivity often gives an effect of disorder, and different readers, as we have seen, cope with this in different ways. The inattentive reader speedily loses his way. The attentive reader must somehow teach himself to read the prose fiction as if it were poetry. Such novels—the works of Dorothy Richardson or of Virginia Woolf—belong to that category of fiction of which T. S. Eliot spoke when he said that "only sensibilities trained on poetry can wholly appreciate" them. By this he meant (what we saw in the testimony of the two women poets about Dorothy Richardson) that the novel is read not as a time-sequence but as a heterogeneous series of perceptions each catching its moment of intensity without reference to what lies on the succeeding pages, but the entire reading of which conveys a poetic synthesis.

In his lecture on *The Three Voices of Poetry*, T. S. Eliot describes how in a given poem we have sometimes the voice of the poet talking to himself, or to nobody; then the voice of the poet may be heard, addressing an audience; while the third voice is that of the poet attempting to create a dramatic character speaking in verse, "when he is saying, not what he would say in his own person, but only what he can say within the limits of one imaginary character addressing another imaginary character." It is this third voice of poetry with which the subjective novel finds itself concerned, the one in which the author tries to disguise his speech so effectively that—like the great actor upon the stage—he becomes someone else.

In the old novels the second voice of Mr Eliot's definition was always heard: the omniscient author was nearly always present and nearly always addressing an audience. Perhaps, for the purposes of fiction, we can put it in another way: in the old novels we are nearly always seated face to face with the author; it is he who is looking out of the window and telling us the story of what he sees. We can see only that which he tells us he sees, and only that which he wants to describe to us. However much we would like to go and take a look out of the window ourselves we cannot do so, because the omniscient author is occupying the choice seat. But he is so marvellous a storyteller—when he knows what he is doing—that he almost makes us forget he is there, and succeeds in weaving his spell over us so that we feel we are looking, with him, at the world beyond the window. And how much he knows of that world! He knows all the intimate secrets of his characters, and what they are thinking at a given moment, and why they act in certain ways—and often he digresses to give us his own moral reflections and his own judgments of the people to whom he has introduced us.

In the psychological novel the author is nowhere in sight. Suddenly *we* are seated at the window. Somewhere, above, behind, below, out beyond the window the author is busy being a stage-manager and an actor, arranging what we shall see. He tries to give us the illusion constantly that we are experiencing what is happening there; and in the process he asks us to look at all sorts of extraneous things, strange things, as if we were in one of our own dreams in which impossible and implausible events occur: magical transformations, return of episodes and people out of forgotten pasts, masses of geography and history that are part of the common heritage of man, a veritable mental cinema of flashing images often confused and incoherent, often sharply-focused, so that, as before, we forget ourselves and have crossed over the window-sill and are ourselves out there amid the confusion, living all that the writer has arranged for us. From being listeners once removed from the scene, we have become actual participants. The effect is to make us use our eyes to see—and to feel what we have seen—rather than to rely upon someone else's report of what *he* has seen. When we stop to think about it, we know that all this has been artfully arranged. And we must face the inevitable truth that the extent of our perception will depend in a marked degree upon our own eyes. The artist, in such a case, can never give us a better pair of eyes than we have. He may sometimes give us tinted glasses, but the perception, the pitch of perception and feeling, is ours, and it is undergoing a curious relationship with *his* expression of reality, his expression of feeling, his perception. It may be that in this process the artist makes unprecedented and unreasonable demands upon us as readers. We must recognize, however, that he forces nothing upon us; it rests with us, if we wish, to make the effort to discover whether communication with him is at all possible. It is not always possible, inevitably; and while this may give a reader a sense of frustration and may sometimes be the fault of the artist, generally it must be recognized rather as a failure of the two consciousnesses involved to establish a harmonious relationship. This happens often enough in life; there is no reason why we may not expect it to happen sometimes in our relationship to certain novels that we read.

The psychological novelist may, also, sometimes take us into certain minds where we do not care to remain. This reflects our taste and feeling and is no reflection on the artist. In life we do not exclusively meet persons agreeable to us. Drawing-rooms are filled with people with whom we do not care to remain. Withdrawal again is always possible. Both readers and critics who have insistently asked the psychological novelist to mend his ways and revert to old methods and old forms have failed to recognize the collaborative nature of novel-reading. The argument advanced by certain of our less perceptive critics, that there was no justification for attempting to discover new techniques to render subjective experience when the traditional mode of narration has so richly served us, is so much an appeal for turning the novel into something rigid and static that it can only be dismissed as puerile.

It is these critics too who have tended to regard the psychological novel as morbid, because it goes into the mind and explores "unhealthy" areas of experience. They often argue that the subjective novel springs from incapacitated persons, Proust and his asthma, Joyce and his near-blindness, Virginia Woolf and her melancholia? Are we being given the abnormal rather than the normal vision of life? Without trying to argue about the word "normal," we can only shrug our shoulders at such failures in critical perception and observe that among the conventional novelists we find also what might be termed "unhealthy" and morbid material, that such material is part of life and that the novelist cannot be legislated into exuding perpetually radiant health and good cheer. We know that the mind at war with itself, and therefore often troubled and sick, can acquire a sharpness of vision that the person enjoying sound health in broad daylight sometimes does not possess. A sense of well-being in a writer does not tend to encourage him to muse upon his fate. The literary artist concerned with broad daylight may not want to look into the dark corners of the night. Indeed, he may be too soundly asleep over a good dinner to be able to do so. But a Marcel Proust, lying awake far into the night, achieves his insight with the aid of his insomnia, and we are the beneficiaries of his suffering. I think that we are concerned not with the state of health of the artist but the art itself. Morbidity *qua* morbidity is not necessarily art; but morbid elements in art do not necessarily vitiate it.

I have said that the novel of subjectivity represents historically a return to romanticism; but it is not a return to the romantic hero. Marcel unravelling his life at Combray, Stephen strutting with his ashplant, Bloom eating the kidney in Eccles Street, Molly submerged in her sexual fantasies—these are hardly the noble, exalted, developed figures of the old novels. Granted we have moved from the open air of Waterloo and the Napoleonic battles on the route to Moscow, into the cork-lined room, the Martello tower, or even the privy in Eccles Street. We touch here on the question whether a figure is diminished in stature because we see it in its more mundane character. It is a little like discussing the actress who has dazzled us on the stage while the lights have played on her and she has embodied radiant youth and beauty, but who in the dressing-room backstage, amid her powders and perfume bottles, with the paint an inch thick on her face, shows her age, and is shorn of all the romance she has created but a few minutes before. Who will deny, however, that the actress performing her dream work before the footlights and the creature of flesh and blood backstage are both parts of reality, and that perhaps to see the actress in her state of confused déshabille backstage as well as the creator of the dream is to understand more richly the difference between illusion and reality, between art and life. I am not sure that each in his own way, the romantic hero, so much an expression of his age, so conscious of the palpitations of his heart, so deeply engrossed in his sensibility, is any different from the more deeply subjective Stephen with his agenbite of inwit, or Marcel seeking to recapture the palimpsest quality of memory.

In 1889 in an essay on the future of the novel, only recently reprinted, Henry James expressed the belief that fiction had a long and rich road before it.

Man rejoices in an incomparable faculty for presently mutilating and disfiguring any plaything that has helped create for him the illusion of leisure; nevertheless, so long as life retains its power of projecting itself upon his imagination, he will find the novel work off the impression better than anything he knows. Anything better for the purpose has assuredly yet to be discovered. He will give it up only when life itself too thoroughly disagrees with him. Even then, indeed, may fiction not find a second wind, or a fiftieth, in the very portrayal of that collapse? Till the world is an unpeopled void there will be an image in the mirror. What need more immediately concern us, therefore, is the care of seeing that the image shall continue various and vivid. . . . So long as there is a subject treated, so long will it depend wholly on the treatment to rekindle the fire.

James was writing when the Stendhalian "image in the mirror" was still literary, that is before photography and its children, the cinema and television, had begun to project images much more elaborate, detailed and "real" than any novelist could ever devise. But now that we have lived half a century into the future of which James was writing, it is clear that the novel form has lost none of its vitality. Certainly the techniques evolved by the psychological novelists, by which they penetrated deeper into realities of the mind, have passed into the common currency of fiction, and there are signs among the younger writers of further refinement of techniques and a moulding of the "stream of consciousness" to new uses as well as an integration of it into the older type of narrated fiction. The novelist knows today that in the portrayal of the mind's atmosphere the literary art has achieved what seemed at one time impossible: Proust's observation of himself, Joyce's matching of language to sound and image, Virginia Woolf's use of poetic imagery, Faulkner's bold sally into the consciousness of an idiot—all these represent victories of literature over the seeming anarchy of life, to be cherished and studied and used. The fundamental law that we have found for all art applies here: that so long as there has been synthesis and refinement, an attempt to achieve an artistic vision of experience and of beauty and a constant search for truth, what has been accomplished has added diversity and richness to the literature of our time. Art is never static. It neither accepts conformity nor does it like repetition. When it is reduced to the status of propaganda, it ceases to be art and becomes advertising. Art thrives best on the variousness of life and on a search for new forms and new techniques. Forms outlive their usefulness; are revived; take on new life. Art can flow into the chaos of surrealism and dada and back again into a beauty more formal and disciplined. It seems to have a way of defying rigidities alike of form and of criticism. Of the art we have examined here we can say that the twentieth-century novel need not hang its head in shame. The vitality of a Proust and a Joyce will suffice for the second half of this century's fiction even if it should prove utterly barren of innovation.

PART II
MODES OF SUBJECTIVITY

CHAPTER I

DIALECTIC OF THE MIND: TOLSTOY

C. P. SNOW, in his criticism of the subjective novel, re-
gretted that fiction in England has a "suicidal tendency
to narrow its range." And he invoked Tolstoy and *War
and Peace* in his argument for the large panoramic novel
which portrays cities, men, battles, life on great estates—
even while the novelist allows himself many pages to
reflect on a discursive theory of historical probability.
Snow however is so occupied in exalting one kind of
novel at the expense of another, that he does not recognize the greatest virtue of the novel-form in English: its
elasticity. An art gallery is not devoted exclusively to
murals and frescoes: there are smaller rooms for minia-
tures, pastels, watercolors. A form which has produced
works as "busy" as *Pickwick* and *Ulysses*, and works as
economical as *A Passage to India* and *Mrs Dalloway*, can
hardly be called "suicidal."

It is a measure of the genius of Tolstoy that he can be
invoked not only for his great murals and his panoramas
of outer reality, but for his close and observant exploration of the subjective life of his characters as well. In certain respects he anticipated Joyce; indeed he may yet
come to be judged as the most significant precursor of
the modern psychological novel and the stream of consciousness. Long before Dujardin, he sought to record
perceptual experience; he was aware of association,
point of view, simultaneity. The difference between him
and Dujardin, on the experimental level, was that he
continued to function as an omniscient author. We remain "outside" his characters; but his picture of their
inner condition has a sharpness and a reality that is very
close to Mrs. Bloom's monologue or Mrs. Dalloway's
reveries in the London streets. The Russian critic

Chernyshevsky, who recognized this early in Tolstoy's work, called it his "dialectic of the mind." Gleb Struve * has shown that this critic was the first to use the term "internal monologue" to characterize the phenomenon. Chernyshevsky's description of the dialectic in Tolstoy, as quoted by Professor Struve, could be applied to any of the subjective novels of our time. Tolstoy, he said, was "interested in observing how an emotion, arising spontaneously from a given situation or impression, and succumbing to the influence of memories and the effect of combinations supplied by imagination, merges into other emotions, returns again to its starting point and wanders on and on along the whole chain of memories; how a thought, born of a primary sensation, is carried on and on, fusing dreams with actual sensations, and anticipations of the future with reflections about the present." This is an admirable statement and does honor to the critic who recognized the problem of subjectivity in fiction even before Tolstoy had written *War and Peace* and *Anna Karenin*.

2

It is possible to discover many passages in Tolstoy illustrative of Chernyshevsky's observations, for the Russian novelist is particularly alert to the life of the senses. In the final chapters of *Anna Karenin*, when Tolstoy wishes to convey the profound despondency of his heroine—in the very last moments of her life—it is to record the vividness with which sights and smells impinge upon her consciousness even while she is retreating in memory to the past, to far-away things that will hide from her the dispersed state of her feelings—her swing from despair to hate, to the wish to obliterate all experience. As she sits in her carriage, aware of its elastic springs and the trot of the horses, she falls to reading the signboards:

Office and warehouse . . . Dental surgeon . . . Yes, I will tell Dolly everything. She doesn't like Vronsky. It will be painful and humiliating, but I'll tell her all about everything. She is fond of me and I will follow her advice. I won't give in to him.

* In his valuable article in PMLA, LXIX, No. 5 (Dec. 1954) 1101–11

148

I won't allow him to teach me . . . Filippov, pastry-cook—
I've heard he sends his pastry to St. Petersburg. The Moscow
water is so good. Ah, the springs at Mitishchen, and the pancakes!

From her tragic love-affair with Vronsky, to taking
counsel with Dolly, her consciousness has shifted (in the
manner of Molly Bloom half a century later) to pastry
and water, to pancakes and the springs of Mitishchen.
And a moment later, as her carriage passes a building:

. . . How nasty that paint smells! Why is it they're always
painting and building? *Dressmaking and millinery*, she read. A
man bowed to her. It was Annushka's husband. Our para-
sites, she remembered the words Vronsky had used. 'Our?'
Why our? What's so dreadful is that one can't tear up the
past by its roots. Yes but I can try not to think of it. I must
do that.

Tolstoy recognized, and his successors were to go still
further, that nothing could convey the anguish of Anna
and her distracted thought more vividly than direct
quotation from her sensory as well as mental experience
at this particular moment. And the smell of paint, the
taste-memory of pastry and springwater, are as relevant
as her remembering what Vronsky said. The state of
diffused consciousness will continue to the moment when
she will let herself fall under the wheels of the train, and
her last thought will be the classic one of psychoanalysis
of a later generation—the self-destruction that is at the
same time destruction of the loved one, "and I shall
punish him and escape from them all and from myself." *

3

In *War and Peace*, which preceded *Anna Karenin*, we
come upon a passage which shows Tolstoy exploring the
hypnagogic state in a manner that Joyce never attempted
in the falling-asleep reverie of Molly Bloom. It occurs
at the moment when Rostov, on picket duty, rides from
post to post; he is exhausted and dozes off constantly
while on his horse. Here Tolstoy is touching upon the
word-condensation and association that will be at the

* The Rosemary Edmonds translation of *Anna Karenin*, in the
Penguin Classics.

heart of Joyce's experiment in *Finnegans Wake*. But he is not concerned in reality with that kind of association, as with capturing the state of "waking-sleep"—the fading of consciousness to the borderland of the unconscious, and the repeated return from that borderland to the actuality of the soldier's task. Rostov has dozed off in the saddle and a shout in the distance rouses him:

"Where am I? Oh yes, in the picket line . . . the pass and watchword: *draught-bar, Olmütz*. What bad luck that our squadron will be in reserve tomorrow . . ." he thought. "I'll ask to go to the front . . ."

and then he sees the gleam of a slope and a black knoll and wonders whether the gleam is that of light on a snow-patch

It must be snow, that patch . . . a patch—*une tache* . . . Natash-a, my sister, black eyes. Na-tash-a . . . (won't she be surprised when I tell her I've seen the Emperor!) Na-tash-a . . . take my *sabretache* . . .

and his reverie is interrupted suddenly, and he stirs from somnolescence to the waking state when the voice of a hussar abruptly tells him to keep to the right—he is heading for bushes. Rostov lifts his head, pulls his horse up. The drowsiness returns:

. . . But, I say, what was I thinking? I mustn't forget. How I shall speak to the Emperor? No, that's not it—that's for tomorrow. Oh yes! Na-tash-a . . . *sabretache* . . . sabre them . . . Whom? The hussars . . . Ah, the hussars with moustaches, and I was thinking about him just opposite Guryev's house . . . Old man Guryev . . . Oh, but Denisov's a fine fellow! No, but that's all nonsense. The great thing now is that the Emperor's here. How he looked at me and longed to say something but dared not . . . No, it was I who did not dare. But that's nonsense, the great thing is not to forget the important thing I was thinking. Yes, Na-tash-a, *sabretache* . . . oh yes, yes. That's it.*

And again his head sinks forward until he seems to hear a shot.

The discontinuity, what we might call the "scrambled data" of stream-of-consciousness writing can be discerned here: and the "trigger" for the refrain of his

* The Rosemary Edmonds translation.

sister's name *Natasha* with the *sabretache* [the leather satchel suspended on the left side by long straps from the sword belt of a cavalry officer], is the *tache*, the white patch on the hillside. Tolstoy has evoked by the simplest means, by the telescoped word within Rostovs's sister's name, consciousness turning back on itself, attempting to think sequentially, and the world of sleep descending between the thoughts.

It might be illuminating by way of contrast to glance, at this point, at the hypnagogic passage in Dujardin's *Les lauriers sont coupés*, to observe how another writer tries to capture the same moment of sleep and waking. This occurs in the scene in which Daniel Prince, alone at last with the actress, places his head on her shoulder, and blissfully passes into a state of semi-wakefulness in his happiness to be near her. The passage is fairly well known, certainly the one which comes closest to stream-of-consciousness. A song is running through Prince's mind

I love my turkeys and my sheep, But oh I love you more . . . That street girl with the bold eyes and cherry lips . . . Soon we will go out under the shadow of the trees, in our ears a distant music . . . *For I love you* . . . *and you love me;* yes, not only *I love you,* but at last *you love me* . . . a kiss now . . . *and you love me.* She is asleep. I'm nearly asleep myself, my eyes half-closed . . . this is her body; the rise and fall of her breast, her blended fragrance, oh lovely April night! . . . . Presently we shall be driving together . . . in the cool air . . . we will go out . . . quite soon . . . the two candles . . . there along the boulevards. . . .*

This does not begin to be as effective as the Tolstoy, perhaps because the Russian gives us a much more dramatic moment. But it shows the pursuit by a writer of the same inner reality. By comparison with these, Molly Bloom's monologue is in reality too wide-awake.

. . . if I can doze off 1 2 3 4 5 what kind of flowers are those they invented like the stars the wallpaper in Lombard street was much nicer the apron he gave me was like that something only I only wore it twice better lower this lamp and try again so as I can get up early I'll go to Lambes there beside Findlaters and get them to send us some glowers

* The Stuart Gilbert translation

151

She does not doze off; and in the final pages of *Ulysses* we accordingly discover one of Joyce's missed opportunities—he who compulsively sought to set himself every possible problem and to find a solution for it.

4

We know that we need not compare a painted landscape to its photograph to discover how well or badly it has been painted. We know equally that if we could monitor a stream of consciousness, we would get a jumble of raw data that would have to be washed out through a sieve, to be used in fiction, as prospectors wash away earth to find gold. Nevertheless, and for the interest of the comparison, I would like to place beside the hypnagogic passages quoted above, the transcription of an actual hypnagogic moment, recorded during recent inquiries into the relationship of induced pre-sleep experience of dreams.* The comparison may prove nothing, but it will show that in their attempts to find words for experiences not always verbal, writers have worked better than they knew. In the laboratory experiment the subject was shown, at the time of his going to bed, a film of a monkey and its dead baby, culminating in the gruesome moment when the animal begins to eat the baby. The experimenters were interested in discovering how such a visual shock can build itself into man's dream-work. What is of interest to us, however, is the tape of the subject's remarks as he was falling asleep. He was asked simply to speak his thoughts; this offers fitful and partial glimpses into consciousness:

I am getting hungrier by the minute. Thinking about food is making me hungry. (*Pause, yawn*) I wonder what time it is. If I stay awake much longer, I'll fall asleep with my eyes open, which would be something. (*Yawn*)

(*long pause*) Mmm . . . well, I'm glad . . . that baby who I saw in that movie. The title of the movie film, "Dead Baby." I was glad that wasn't a human baby. I don't think I really liked that

* Drs. Herman A. Witkin and Helen B. Lewis, "The Relation of Experimentally Induced Pre-Sleep Experience to Dreams." (Psychology Laboratory, Department of Psychiatry, State University of New York Downstate Medical Center, January 1964.

scene there . . . that one wasn't bad . . . I wonder what the monkey was thinking about . . . If it was thinking about anything. (*pause*) Seems like it was trying to bring it back to life. I wonder if it knew it was dead. If it knew it was a baby. (*pause*) Well, anyway it was an interesting movie . . . (*pause*) I wish I could go to sleep now. It must be after 11 by now. Or almost 11. I can probably get along all right on six hours, five hours of sleep. I wonder how I'll have a chance to get a nap tonight. See faces. If I imagine hard enough drawings of faces. Just lines. No shading, just lines. Drawings. Line drawings. Very good. Wish I could do almost as well. I hear voices. I wonder if somebody's in here. Suppose maybe there are. When I close my eyes everything turns blue. Blue-gray. Like uh . . like . . . I almost see a waterfall . . . a blue waterfall. Open my eyes, I close my eyes, I see a blue waterfall. I open my eyes I see a red sky with a . . dark . . black . . clouds. When I close my eyes I see . . . I don't know . . . leaves . . . a pattern of leaves, and then it disappears. There's a pool, long green pool with stones in . . . stones at the bottom of a clear blue pool. I open my eyes and it disappears. I close my eyes . . . what's this . . . Ha . . looks like a frog . . . blue-green frog, with dark gray spots. I open my eyes and they're gone. Close my eyes I see a lot of things. Baby . . . and what's this. . . . (*sound of regular breathing, slight snore.*)

This passage from life is illuminating; and art could improve it without diminishing its authenticity. For what Joyce and Faulkner and Mrs. Woolf have done—and Tolstoy before them—has been simply to infuse their personal poetry into the often turgid data of consciousness. One of the limitations of Joyce has been that he has gloried a little too much in turgidity; but we can imagine how Faulkner might use the blue waterfall in this passage or "the stones at the bottom of a clear blue pool." And we know what delicate moments of perception Virginia Woolf would find in "a pattern of leaves, and then it disappears" or the "blue-green frog, with dark grey spots." There is no simultaneity here; otherwise the passage conforms to the given point of view within present time, and there is a kind of associative logic in its discontinuity. Mysterious is the dialectic of the mind; and it requires the mysterious process of poetry—as our "subjective" novelists have shown—to render it.

CHAPTER II

DOROTHY RICHARDSON'S
PILGRIMAGE

THE DEATH of Dorothy Miller Richardson at eighty-four in 1957, in England, removed from the literary scene the last of the experimenters who in the century's opening years created the "inside-looking-out" novel—what we more commonly speak of as the "stream of consciousness" novel. The least read and the most unobtrusive of the experimenters, she had outlived them all, outlived, indeed, her own work and her own modest reputation. Proust, on his side of the Channel, had died at the dawn of the nineteen twenties, Virginia Woolf and James Joyce, during the first years of the Second World War. Miss Richardson lived on for the better part of two decades. But she added no new works. The twelfth section or "chapter" of her novel was published in 1938, three years before the deaths of Joyce and Mrs. Woolf. From a literary point of view it was as if she had died with them. The irony was that she survived to see from the quiet of her own oblivion the growth of the Joyce legend, the posthumous successes of Mrs. Woolf.

Her long novel marked the beginning of a movement in English fiction and extended over the years to the point where it may have also marked its completion. But long before this, literary criticism threw up its hands in weary bafflement or rude dismissal; and literary history bids fair to use *Pilgrimage* not so much for its exploration of the inner consciousness as for its vivid portraits of certain identifiable figures and its reflection of a certain era in English life and letters. For it is also, to a degree, a *livre à clé* and certain readers have already recognized the marked resemblance between Hypo Wilson and H. G. Wells. Indeed one of Wells's biographers testifies that the novelist's portrait in *Pilgrimage* is "three-dimensional," revealing "the inner Wells as no letter, book, or talk ever could." He adds that Miss Richardson's portrait represents "a fusion of many years' friendship with the intuitive eye of the artist; it is Wells stripped of his many masks."

But this is a matter for Wells's biographer and for Miss Richardson's. For criticism the questions *Pilgrimage* raised remain to be fully answered. By the tenets of the "new criticism" the novel fails as a work of art because we become involved in the so-called "affective fallacy"; that is, we find ourselves discussing the reader as much as the work, his empathy with the single character and his capacity to enter into the novel. Since the work is written from the "inside" one either is able to move into the heroine's consciousness or is incapable of reading—or "experiencing"—the book. This would seem to be the long and the short of it. And since many of the book's critics seemed unaware of this, we find ourselves involved in large failures in empathy: gross failures to grasp the essence of Miss Richardson's curious and obsessive application of the Jamesian theory of the "point of view."

This would explain the critical bafflement and the rude dismissals.

2

But in the critical history of *Pilgrimage* there were certain exceptions. John Cowper Powys, long ago, with what seemed excessive enthusiasm, invoked Goethe and Wordsworth, and described *Pilgrimage* as a "stupendous achievement," and Graham Greene discerned the life and force in the book while confessing to the tedium of its "monstrous subjectivity." Words such as *stupendous* and *monstrous* suggest a certain critical ambivalence, and similar extremes may be found among the literary historians. Of two histories of the writing of our time recently perused, one devoted five close analytical pages to Miss Richardson, the other breathed not a word, not even a "for the record" footnote, about her. In 1920 Virginia Woolf could couple Miss Richardson with Joyce—everyone did; in 1948 Stanley Edgar Hyman, overlooking literary history, reproached Ezra Pound for "yoking . . . a great writer and an inferior one." Times change; judgments change; and the verdict on Miss Richardson seems to be that she was a misguided pioneer who set out, all unaware of Proust, to do something in England akin to *A la recherche du temps perdu*—but paralleled Proust's quest rather than his achievement.

Certainly there can be no question of placing her now on an equality of footing with Proust and Joyce. Miss Richardson was a journeyman beside the nimble-minded Irishman, nor did she have the Frenchman's capacity for discovering a universe in a perfume. She must be written down rather as one of the hardy and plodding experimenters of literature, the axe-swingers and stump-pullers, those who have a single moment of vision which suffices for a lifetime. There was a kind of Zola in Miss Richardson, not in her work but in herself as the artist-type—the immense recording of data, the observation and introspection and note-taking, the carrying out of a major project according to plan. *Pilgrimage* is not a Rougon Macquart, but it is a long and detailed progress through the mind and emotions of an English girl who emerges from a Victorian adolescence and attains maturity and liberation in the early decades of our century. To re-read Miss Richardson now and to re-appraise her in her four thick volumes which embody her twelve novels or "chapters," is to marvel at her unflagging zeal: the book is a victory of resolution, patience, and sensibility over limited artistic means. *Pilgrimage* for all its sprawling minuteness, its endless internal monologue sensitively alert to sunlight and shadow, London streets and rooms, contains distinct qualities of strength, insight and feeling, and above all vitality—the vitality of a purposeful individual who cannot be swerved from a creative task, who indeed converts the task into self-education as a woman and an artist.

That task Miss Richardson long ago defined for us. She did not like the strong male ego which she often encountered in English fiction. She offered instead a novel designed to reveal the feminine sensibility (we might call it the feminine ego) "from the inside." At the same time she recognized that a novelist nearly always writes or re-writes the book of himself. Like Proust, like Joyce, she quarried her material within her personal consciousness: and like her famous fellow-writers, she concerned herself not with telling the story of her experience in the old-fashioned circumstantial way, but through human per-ception—the use of her senses, and by seeking to re-capture the data to be found in the examination of any moment of our lives. Thanks to the careful searches of Gloria Glikin we now know much more about Miss Rich-ardson and how she designed and carried out her work. Dr. Glikin's essay * illustrates the uses of literary history in the study of the novel. For when a novel is subjective, it is in some form or other, autobiographical. It is auto-biography depersonalized. And if the life behind it is, from one point of view, irrelevant for the study of the creative imagination, it has also a singular relevance. As the *Portrait of the Artist as a Young Man* is not wholly a por-trait of Joyce the young man, but is a very vivid portrait of the artist in Joyce, so there is a portrait of a human be-ing in *Pilgrimage*, and this portrait is painted in the cham-bers of Dorothy Richardson's life. One can now under-stand, for instance, what brought Miss Richardson and H. G. Wells, together; how her work was her way of over-coming the stigma of her shopkeeper class, as Wells sought to overcome the sense of inferiority he felt be-cause his parents were servants. A democratic America may find it difficult to understand British Victorian class hierarchies; yet the cult of D. H. Lawrence owes its force to this very fact: the lady must sleep with the game-keeper. The aristocracy must receive a transfusion from the lower classes.

Dorothy Richardson should be read not only as a brave experimenter of the Joycean era, but as a woman who documented the struggle later taken up by Britain's angry young men. Her novel—which Leslie Fiedler finds "so palely *dully*" (hers is "the least acceptable of dullness"

* "Dorothy M. Richardson: The Personal 'Pilgrimage,' " PMLA LXXVIII No. 5, 586–600 (December 1963)

he says) is filled with interest for anyone wishing to know Victorian and Edwardian English middle-class life and the conditioned middle-class emotion; and it is at the same time a curious picture of low-bohemia and the vanished world of the teapot rebels and the Fabians; and the Edwardian "social-consciousness." Dullness is a relative matter: and there are many pages in *Ulysses* in which we may feel we are reading not a novel but a telephone directory. Miss Richardson has painted a valid self-portrait. She wanted it to be the only surviving portrait of her and to that end she concealed all the "facts" of her life. Her entry in *Who's Who* during her lifetime gave neither place of birth nor date. She furnished only a list of her books. There was something exemplary in her desire to displace life by art. But while this is possible in poetry, it is not altogether possible in fiction, where the mirror in the roadway catches many images of time and place, not least the visage of the novelist himself, or at least some reflection of his temperament. Miss Richardson's visage is first that of a seventeen-year old: and we take our leave of her at forty in the twelfth section. But even when her four-volume novel was announced as "complete," she was at work on a thirteenth section, a kind of ending that would bring her heroine to the moment when she begins writing her novel. As Proust showed, this kind of novel is capable, even within tight organization and structure, of continual expansion so long as the beginning and end are clearly established.

3

Miss Richardson's mode of subjectivity was not "stream-of-consciousness." She did not care for William James's metaphor, and did not attempt to render the flow of thought. She employed at first a filtered indirect internal monologue which, as she advanced into the work, becomes increasingly direct in its notation of thought and perception. With "simultaneity" she had no concern: nor with the scrambling of her materials. Her method is often Jamesian in its withholding of anything the heroine does not perceive or sense. She remains closer to the center than the periphery of consciousness.

Miss Richardson's problem, with critics and with her audience, resides in the relationship required between the reader and her book. If one is caught up in the conveyed consciousness, one ends by seeing and hearing in her particular way; and the reader has the uncanny feeling of being in someone else's skin. As my earlier chapter shows, I have conducted an informal inquiry among Richardson readers; the following was recorded for me by one woman who read *Pilgrimage* a few years ago:

... it is strange how I am forced to experience things as she does, and yet how I, as the reader, maintain my own reactions to both the shared experience and her behavior, so that I am *literally* an individual trapped in her mind, alternately enjoying life through her body and mind and wanting to scream because I must do so. Her solutions often take an alien path for me, but I can see why they make sense for her. Where our interests and inclinations agree, she takes me into a delightful peace and enjoyment; when she half senses, but turns away from warm, rough masculine qualities, she leaves me thoroughly frustrated. I've experienced British femininity, repeated and drilled in and taught me through dozens of unrelated experiences, and I've been obliged to relate to any number of men I don't want to, and not relate to any number of men I rather liked. When she has her affair with Hypo, for example, I experience the whole ridiculous business (ridiculous to me, not to Miriam) and when she finally "falls" for a French girl, takes her as a room-mate and is charmed by the aggressive femininity of the girl, I am really irritated beyond measure to suffer such an overt homosexual approach while my twin—Miriam—can't see beyond the end of her nose what she is doing.

This candid glimpse of the delights and irritations of reading subjective fiction hardly suggests "dullness." To be sure, the heroine swallows too many impressions whole; nevertheless Miss Richardson conveys a close picture of environment. She is a writer of bulk and of concreteness. In the early pages of the novel things are sharply seen and people are blurred. As one moves farther along, and the heroine grows older, people begin to emerge more clearly. The characters do not develop; but the heroine's perception of them does.

Pilgrimage, like most internal monologue novels, has no story, no plot, and no characters. Graham Greene admirably summarizes: "There is no longer a Miss Richardson: only Miriam—Miriam off to teach English in a German school, off again to be a teacher in North London, a governess in the country, a dental secretary in Wimpole Street; a flotsam of female friendships piling up, descriptions of clothing, lodgings, encounters at the Fabian Society" and so on through her first adventure on a bicycle, her intellectual friendships with men, her difficulties with sex, and her struggles to understand herself in a dense and pervasive London. In the novel we learn how Miss Richardson discovered *The Ambassadors* (Miriam reads it with intense excitement) and learned from Henry James the proper use of "point of view." The fascination of putting the reader into a given angle of vision and keeping him there: this was the lesson of the Master for Miss Richardson and she learned it well; it became the guiding light by which she worked:

The train was high above the platform. Politely smiling, Miriam scrambled to the window. The platform was moving, the large bright station moving away. Fraülein's wide smile was creasing and caverning under her hat from which the veil was thrown back . . . Fraülein's form flowed slowly away with the platform.

Today we would call this the "camera eye," so accustomed are we to seeing it done in the cinema. Miss Richardson anticipated the moving picture camera; indeed, we now know how deeply she studied and wrote about the movies. From the first she brought everything into the orbit of Miriam's eyes and her senses and sought to capture within a book the *ewige Weibliche*—not as men might express it, but as women experienced it. In undertaking to write "point of view" on so large a scale, Miss Richardson set herself a much more difficult task than Proust. One wonders indeed what the French writer might have done with such a method had he elected to use it instead of the autobiographical "I."

The true difficulty of *Pilgrimage* lies in its density. Readers of both sexes are asked to establish rapport with two thousand pages containing the flotsam and jetsam of consciousness, fragments of experience, emotions conveyed in emotion-limiting words. A reader can easily achieve a relation with a novel when he is on the outside, watching the story unfold; it is another matter to be "on the inside" looking out—and especially "on the inside" of an adolescent girl, in the first sections. This explains why the successful reading of the book seems to depend in a considerable measure on the reader's sex and on his capacity for identification and "transference." Usually it is the women who speak of Miss Richardson's achievement as "uncanny" and filled with "intensities." Men often find it difficult to meet her requirement that they become the adolescent Miriam of *Pointed Roofs* and grow up with her in the succeeding volumes.

Few men—few critics of their sex—have been willing to climb into Miss Richardson's boat; the journey is long, the "stream of consciousness" difficult—raw unabstracted data, the absence of the omniscient author to serve as guide, the consequent need to become the author so as to bring some order into the great mass of feminine experience offered us; and then the need, Orlando-like, to become the girl or woman, to become Miriam if we are to be her consciousness. Few writers have placed so double-weighted a burden upon their readers. And yet if the challenge is met and the empathy achieved, Dorothy Richardson offers us, on certain pages, a remarkable emotional luminescence—as well as, historically speaking, a record of the trying out of a new technique, the opportunity to examine a turning point in the modern English novel. There is a distinct possibility that a new generation of readers—if there will continue to be readers at all—may truly discover Dorothy Richardson for the first time.

CHAPTER III

HOW TO READ
THE SOUND AND THE FURY *

THE OPENING PAGES of *The Sound and the Fury* take us into a bewildering world, as if we were traversing without pause the ages of man—and in the wrong order. The seasons merge and blur; disembodied voices speak to us; we participate in a dance of the senses. Old sensations are evoked: the brightness of certain days, dancing sunlight and leaping firelight, the smell of damp leaves, the hard, cold frostiness of winter. It is April, bright grass and green; and the next moment it is Christmas. There are caddies on a golf course, and there is a girl named Caddy. Benjy is thirty-three, but he is also three, or thirteen. Certain pages remind us of Joyce's artist-as-a-baby and the moocow coming down the road. The click of Benjy's sensory memory seems to be accompanied by the click of the linotype: long passages are given in alternation, first in roman type and then in italic. The editors of the *Modern Library* rightly feared that frustrated readers might hurl the book away in anger; but when they asked Faulkner to write an explicatory preface, he wrote an Appendix instead. So much for publishers who want artists to explain their art! If we read this Appendix, where one usually reads the preface, we enter the book so to speak by a back door. And Faulkner's genealogy of the Compson family only increases our confusion. But to explain technique and discuss the form of the novel was foreign to Faulkner and his intuitive art. Moreover, it would have involved telling the reader what he must, in the end, discover for himself. And what he must discover, above all, in such a book as *The Sound and the Fury*, is a new way of reading fiction.

* Reprinted from *Varieties of Literary Experience*, edited by Stanley Burnshaw. Copyright, 1962, by New York University Press.

A new way of reading fiction. For obviously, when the material is offered to the reader not in the old, neat, ordered, narrated form, packaged, so to speak, chapter by chapter, but comes to him higgledy-piggledy, it is at this scrambled story that he must look—unless he starts to re-fashion the book. Indeed such a thing has happened: two teachers in California, gathering round them their little flock of seminar students, did try to take the Benjy section of this novel apart and to re-assemble it in a traditional way. They drew a map of the terrain; they numbered the "levels" of narration both alphabetically and numerically, and they concluded that this section "was consciously constructed as a puzzle or a mystery story, or both combined." Otherwise, they said (with the assurance of the clockmaker looking at all the parts of his clock on the worktable), "otherwise it would seem impossible that the scattered and often brief units could be conclusively placed in the whole structure." A little sober thought suggests that the method of the clockmaker is not applicable here. Faulkner may have enjoyed mystifying the reader; novelists usually are supposed to do that; but he was not constructing a wilful puzzle. It is not in his nature, for one thing, to build labyrinths: in this he differs markedly from Joyce. Moreover, a scrutiny of the text itself, and the author's design which it reveals, makes it amply clear that the "brief units" need not necessarily be consistent with the whole structure. We are concerned here, after all, with consciousness, and with the portrayal of consciousness; moreover, it is the consciousness of an idiot, a man of thirty-three, whose faculties were arrested before he was three—if one can speak here of his having "faculties." And consciousness, even in persons of sanity, for all its brave attempts to find order in the world, is a great confusion of moments of experience, unsorted memories, an intricate organ-board of sensory impressions, playing into areas of clarity and lucidity.

The first problem to be solved in reading this novel is how to cope with the scrambled materials. They *are* scrambled, beyond a doubt; and any hope of recovering whole eggs from the omelette must be set aside at once. Our new way of reading invites us to accept the material in its unsorted unchronological heterogeneous state: it stipulates that we must not try, like the energetic California teachers, to impose conventional order upon it. Our obligation is rather to perceive it *in its disorder*, as Faulkner placed it before us.

The material of Benjy's consciousness is given to us, if we patiently read our text, in terms of his own perceptions and as they come to him. He smells things and people; he often experiences visual objects as if they were odors; he bellows when the unfamiliar crosses his path. We are dealing, in other words, with a three-year-old for whom the world is a safe and neat place only when the *known* things of existence are encountered; otherwise there is discomfort and often anxiety and terror. His world is the world of stimulus and response: and when certain things happen which have happened before, these melt together. Each memory recalls another and enfolds it, probably to "trigger" still another. Benjy snags his clothes on the nail at the golf course in April, when he is with Luster: presently we learn that he snagged them also at some long-ago Christmastime when he was with Caddy. Happening piles upon happening. In the timeless world of Benjy, past and present become one, this moment, and no other. It is Christmas, it is Easter, they are all one. He is thirteen on one page and thirty-three on the next. It is possible to set down a rough chronology, if one wishes: but to what purpose? The story is supposed to come to us as it happens to Benjy. This is what Faulkner intended.

Indeed, when an author elects to tell us a story in this fashion, it would seem logical to follow him in his premises and not to construct new ones. In accepting the material in its scrambled state and seeking to understand it, we are invited by Faulkner to place ourselves within the angle of vision or perception of Benjy; we are involved with *point of view*. We are maneuvered by the novelist into taking over all of Benjy's senses: his eyes become our eyes, his sense of smell is ours, his unique experience of the world around him is our experience for the duration of the book. We are, so to speak, on the inside of an idiot —looking out—even though we retain, at the same time, our own reason and our own awareness. A peculiar empathy is asked of us.

The room went away, but I didn't hush, and the room came back and Dilsey came and sat on the bed, looking at me.

In Benjy's world rooms come to him and go away; the lawn approaches and he walks; the bowl comes up to his mouth and he eats. He is the center of the universe. And when the horse and buggy drives to the left of the statue, instead of to the right, everything suddenly is not in its Benjy-ordered place: façade and cornice, doorway and window, post and tree, are reversed, they flow from right to left. Terror seizes him and he sets up a howl that reverberates through the square. Then, when Jason restores his usual world to him and drives the buggy to the right of the statue, buildings and objects resume their familiar aspect, and Benjy, clutching his broken narcissus, can subside into his staring quiet. Everything now flows from left to right, "each in its ordered place." *

"Each in its ordered place." Exegetes of the Benjy section have for years made much of this "order"—but the order which Faulkner invokes here is simply the compulsive idiot order of Benjy's world, a world of innocence and childishness, of someone who, as Faulkner has said, was mindless from birth, as blank and blind as the empty eyes of the Confederate soldier in the square in Jefferson, round which Luster had driven the horse and buggy the wrong way. The "order," in other words, is the order of Benjy's familiar blind world; we will never understand it if we introduce into it a new kind of order, the order of our own perceiving world.

What Faulkner has achieved in this section has been a significant change in novel-dimension. I refer not only to the technique, nor to the poetry: it is his assimilation,

* "We have attempted to work out why things should be flowing in that special direction and have failed to determine why," say the searchers for the egg-in-the-omelette, in their article in *American Literature* (Vol. XXIX; No. 4, January 1958), "unless [they add] the author is speaking in cryptic terms about his book itself and the smooth flow of type from left to right?"

in a remarkably intuitive fashion, of the lesson of Joyce and of the French Symbolists: for he shows us how a novelist, or a poet, can use language to evoke more perceptions and feelings than unilinear prose has been hitherto accustomed to doing. We can perhaps make a useful analogy with what the impressionist painters and the abstractionists have achieved in our time. They have given us a new way of looking at impressions and abstractions, substituting their vision for the familiar representation of the things we see. With painting or sculpture, as Lessing long ago observed, we are capable of grasping visually—and continuing to observe—what is before our eyes. With words, as with music, we are involved in the double-process of remembering as well as grasping, since a page of printed symbols can never be a picture, or an image. It can only evoke images; it is a way of stimulating our own sensory apparatus.

The new way of reading, then, in prose fiction, is much more complex than the new ways of looking at plastic art. Not only must we take our bearings among the scrambled data, and experience them in terms of our own sensory world, while trying to imagine ourselves into the world of Benjy, but we must in the end deduce story and character, aspect and scene, from information given us in this disordered fashion. That information has included the words spoken to the character by other characters, and the occasional aid given by the intrusive author. We have, in effect, been thrown bodily into scene and into narrative; the author has withdrawn, as in a play, to allow us to figure things out for ourselves. He has placed us neither in a labyrinth nor a puzzle: we are merely in an unfamiliar landscape, as if we had journeyed to a foreign country, and we are asked to use Benjy's eyes and ears and nose, indeed all his senses, as well as our own to determine where we are.

Writing, word by word and sentence by sentence, yet no longer in the old neat chronological order of traditional novelists, Faulkner achieves in the Benjy section an unusual act of "extrapolation." Neither he nor anyone has ever been inside the consciousness of an idiot;

somehow—perhaps by observation of the behavior of half-wits, by deduction and inference, and his own experience of states of childhood—the novelist has been able to create for us the illusion of what the idiot state might be, the helpless, baffled world of pleasant and unpleasant sounds and smells and color impressions, the calm and the terror which the idiot himself can articulate only in animal sound, for Benjy lives in a wordless world. It is Faulkner who supplies the words. He is the scribe-poet-interpreter. And with patience, and the use of our own sensory imagination, we can gradually begin to feel Benjy's world as we become aware that we are reading an exquisite bit of poetic imagining.

Father went to the door and looked at us again. Then the dark came back, and he stood black in the door, and then the door turned black again. Caddy held me and I could hear us all, and the darkness, and something I could smell. And then I could see the windows, where the trees were buzzing. Then the dark began to go in smooth, bright shapes, like it always does, even when Caddy says that I have been asleep.

This *sounds* as if Benjy really comprehends. But it is Faulkner who is putting this world into words. A voice is given to the voiceless.

2

In the foregoing, we have by no means exhausted the complexity of this new way of reading. We know that we are concerned with discontinuity and point of view. Step by step, as we determine what happens in accepting this unsorted, disarranged world and the given angle of vision, we are forced to recognize that other things occur. The language may be set down word-by-word and paragraph-by-paragraph, but Faulkner is busily creating also an illusion of simultaneity: we are hearing, smelling, seeing *at the same time*, as in life. The effect he achieves resembles that of movie-montage where the rapidity of the images, and the sequence in which they come before the eyes, create a multiple activity of the senses and an illusion of things occurring at the same time instead of successively. It is much simpler to do this with pictures than with words. The effect of simultaneity in a novel can be achieved only by the way in which words are grouped and verbal images juxtaposed. Flaubert did this originally in the celebrated fair scene in *Madame Bovary;* Joyce, emulating Flaubert, achieved certain spectacular effects by his verbal audacities in *Ulysses.* Faulkner follows the example of these masters with great skill. The helpful voice chimes in at the moment Benjy watches the firelight or captures a smell. And the other simultaneities operate as a further scrambling process.

In the attempt to give us a sense of simultaneity, resides the author's awareness that he is working in a changed time-dimension. In fiction we have usually found ourselves in the past, listening to an historical narrative. The devices employed in *The Sound and the Fury* are designed, on the other hand, to convey the immediate. Time in such novels may be described as being vertical instead of horizontal. To be sure, Faulkner has dated each section and it is always a specific day in the past. His labels are those of clock and calendar time. Yet when we read, we have the illusion that we are inside his personages, thinking their thoughts, having their perceptual experiences, *at the very moment that these occur,* and these moments are moments of psychological or human time. We all know the difference between the clock and that individual timepiece which exists within us. The clock is, as Faulkner calls it, an "arbitrary dial." It is arbitrary because our inner clock is even more arbitrary: the latter can make a moment seem like a day, or a day a moment; it sometimes makes our winters seem long and our summers short. An hour spent in a traffic jam can seem longer than a whole day on a ski-slope. In *The Sound and the Fury,* Faulkner is concerned at every turn with this difference. And with keeping us in the present, a continuous present. We think the thoughts of the character at the moment that they emerge into his consciousness; and into this present come memories out of the past, which then fall back into the hidden part of consciousness where the old impressions are gathered and stored, to be reawakened in some future present, often in an involuntary fashion, as Proust reawakened Combray within himself at the taste of the cake dipped in the cup of tea. We are in April 7, 1928, when Benjy and Luster are at the golf course, as the label at the beginning tells us; and Luster makes us aware of the immediate in his search for the twenty-five cent piece which will take him, if he finds it, to the circus. For Benjy, on the other hand, the date-label is meaningless. In his mindlessness, neither timepiece nor calendar exist; only that dumb period of childhood when we have our first primitive encounters with sensation, upon which a curtain of knowledge sooner or later descends—never to be fully raised again. The curtain however has never dropped for Benjy. The only love and understanding he can discover is that of his sister Caddy and his relation to her is that of a dumb animal to a human.

In the second section of the novel we are with Benjy's brother at Harvard. It is June 2, 1910, eighteen years *before* the first section; and we follow Quentin Compson from the moment he awakens on the day he has decided to kill himself and tears the hands from his father's watch in an attempt to forget time.

Finally, in the third section, dated April 6, 1928 (the day *before* the Benjy section) we run the little rat-maze of the third brother's life, and experience the sordid and mean world of Jason Compson—up and down his three or four city blocks in Jefferson, Mississippi. His world is a world of fury. His life is driven by a consuming rage.

Thus during three different days, the first two in Easter week of 1928 and the third almost two decades earlier, Faulkner has confined us in the consciousness of each of three members of the Compson family. Through them we have come to know the parents, the sister Caddy, who holds them together in love and hate, her daughter Quentin (named after the Harvard student who died in 1910), and other personages. We have come to know the family as three of its members experienced it and always through their individual perceptions. It is only in the fourth section, dated April 8, 1928 (the day *after* Benjy snagged himself beside the golf course), that the reader emerges from the inner vision of the three brothers into the light of external day. Instead of listening to the monologue of the personages, as we have been doing, we are listening to the voice of the narrator who has finally arrived upon the scene. At last we are concerned with objective, as distinct from subjective, reality: Dilsey's Easter morning.

3

In our daily lives we are confined—from beginning to end—within a single consciousness, our own. We can never find our way into the consciousness of another. We may obtain fitful glimpses into it, but that is all: we have only the barest sense of someone else's experience. We can never know the thoughts of another, save as he tells them to us, or as we deduce them. He may describe them in the sentence-by-sentence way in which we communicate with one another; or we may guess from the expression on his face or the gesture, or other tell-tale signs. But we seldom can be aware of more than this. It is impossible to capture fully the complex, chromatic, radiation of image, sound, fantasy, memory, association, sensation, within our own selves, let alone within another. We employ a loose and picturesque phrase, William James's metaphor, *stream of consciousness*, and remember that he described the attempt to capture some part of this swiftly flowing stream as "turning on the gaslight" to see what the darkness looks like. And yet in *The Sound and the Fury*, by Faulkner's method of telling his story, we have been taken into regions of experience not otherwise visitable: we have been inside the thought-flow or sentience of three persons other than ourselves, and one of them an idiot. It is all illusion, of course: but we have paid our visit through the empathy, artistic sensibility, imaginative construction, and the use of verbal imagery, with which Faulkner imparts life to his interior vision. This is the remarkable achievement of this book.

To accomplish this we have assumed a strenuous task, but a challenging one: that challenge which Virginia

170

Woolf expressed when she asked novelists to set down for us not mere "story," but the "shower of innumerable atoms," in our daily lives: to reveal the simultaneities of experience contained within any moment of a day, with peripheral awareness (as we listen, say, to what is being said to us, but suddenly are aware that we are hearing also the flutter of a window-blind and the low murmur of traffic, and several other voices, and the cough of a motor) even while we are attentively following the reasoning of the speaker, and evaluating what he is saying. If we are capable of this, we must recognize that we may be capable of as much or more in the very act of reading: that it is possible to deal *actively* with narrative material presented to us, rather than merely to listen to a story, as the old authors encouraged us to do. It is true that the richness of their voices and the witchery of their tale-telling sufficed. Faulkner's witchery consists in providing the ground and setting the stage for an unusual act of collaboration with the reader. He does a great deal of "arranging" and it requires unusual technical resources. His book is a supreme example of a work of art in which technique and substance are one.

The active reading which Faulkner asks of us involves our determining for ourselves what the people in this novel are like. The old novelists never left us in doubt; as each character came on the scene he was introduced, pictured, described; and then, in the light of this given knowledge, we could watch him act himself out. In the subjective novels of Joyce, Faulkner, Virginia Woolf, or in a novel such as H. D.'s *Palimpsest* or Conrad Aiken's *Blue Voyage*, the characters reveal themselves by their thoughts and by what they say; we learn to know them as we know people in our daily lives—through observation on our side, and self-revelation on theirs.

When we have read *The Sound and the Fury* we have thus been given a picture of the consciousness of three members of a family, and by this process a picture of the family itself—a declining family in a decaying South. But the picture is wholly subjective. At the end, therefore, Faulkner decided to intervene to complete the story for us in such a manner as would make it possible for us to verify our observations. He accordingly gave us his account of Dilsey, the Negro housekeeper in the Compson family, and it is rendered wholly from the outside. We are never in her thoughts. We see her merely going about her work, knowing her affairs, and helping to link together the lost Southern family. Dilsey knows what time it is. The Negro in the South can ill afford to forget the clock. The Compson clock chimes a certain hour, but she always adds three hours to arrive at exact clock-time. It is indeed later than the Compsons know. Dilsey knows the time of the day and therefore she alone is truly in touch with the real and the immediate. In this way Faulkner symbolizes not only the decay of the Southern gentry, but the fantasy-world of the South for which only the past has had reality. Quentin indeed cannot go on living because what is real to him is a dream of incest in adolescence springing from love for his sister, which has no relation to his adult life. The burden of his imagined guilt springs, as Faulkner observes in his Appendix, from the fact that Quentin "loved not the idea of the incest which he could not commit, but some presbyterian concept of its eternal punishment: he, not God, could by that means cast himself and his sister both into hell, where he could guard her forever and keep her forevermore intact amid the eternal fires." Jason, on his side, is a clumsy, sordid, cunning individual, living by his wits, but always so cunning as to outwit himself. He is the embodiment of a kind of instinctual self-frustrative evil.

Innocence, guilt, evil—each Compson brother in his own way symbolizes the moral world of Southern Calvinism; but he also symbolizes the way in which family tension and social tension mould an individual. The slowly crumbling gentry, selling their land and cultivating a decorum no longer in tune with their world, can end only by divesting themselves of their patrimony and destroying themselves, either literally, as Quentin did, or through a gradual process of self-undermining, as in Jason. The whining helpless mother, the charming but futile resignedly-philosophical father, are the victims of a stagnation they cannot overcome. Their idiot son, in his eerie world, epitomizes the futility of all their lives. *The Sound and the Fury* as a novel expresses all the mortal frustration and questioning of Shakespeare's soliloquy which gives the book its title. It is indeed a tale—a tale of great intensity—told by an idiot, and in the end signifying nothing, motion without purpose. The sound of Benjy and the fury of Jason, the innocence, guilt, and evil in this family is set by Faulkner into Easter week, where all is expiated and washed clean, and man may hope for resurrection and recovery. In this world Dilsey alone has her task and her bearings. She alone knows how to speak to Jason, and to soothe Benjy, and she will take the idiot to the Easter service believing that some Divine illumination will enter his uncomprehending body and penetrate his timeless being.

Such a novel is well described as a Symbolist novel, because the entire work is made to symbolize for us consciousness and the South: in giving us the imaged memories and the tortured inner life of a family Faulkner has given us the tortured inner life of a society which this family represents; and in using language evocatively, Faulkner has been able to make that language convey intensities of feeling and states of consciousness which words can never begin to describe. The world of William Faulkner, in this novel, is not a world of reason or intelligence or rational order. Faulkner proclaims neither order nor disorder. Certainly the "order" of Benjy is hardly rational. The novelist's concern is with feeling. The very title implies it. The sound is anguish and the fury is a manifestation of a kind of primordial animal rage: and this book is about the anguish of the innocent and the fury of the frustrated and the damned. These are the larger meanings we can read in this fiction when we have mastered its difficulties. And it is only through such complexities that Faulkner conveys to us the chaos of the Compson world in a fashion closer to human experience than any mere recital of the Compson's family history. We come to know it because we have been confronted by intensities of feeling rather than recitals of fact.

There exists a short story about the Compson family,
written by Faulkner some time after the novel, which
throws a retrospective light on the book. It is called
"That Evening Sun Go Down" and it is a tale of childish innocence playing itself out on the margin of adult
terror. In this story we see Quentin, Jason, and Caddy
when they are children. Their personalities are formed:
little Quentin is the uncertain and sentient being we will
meet at Harvard; Caddy is kindness and empathy; and
Jason, a mere toddler, is already a little tale-telling rat.
The story deals with Nancy, who has been temporarily
replacing Dilsey in the Compson kitchen. She has been
raped by a white man and is to have a child. Her husband has vowed that he will kill her and leave her body
in the ditch near their hut. As each day's sun goes down
Nancy fears the worst; and in the episode narrated in the
tale she entices the children to her hut and plays games
with them to fend off the terrible moment when she must
face the night alone—and the prospect of her doom. In
the midst of this the children go about their games aware
that Nancy acts strangely, but preoccupied with their
world and the assertion of their diminutive egos. They
are oblivious of the adult drama; we never know whether
Nancy was killed and left in a ditch for the vultures, as
she feared. The story is concerned with the children, and
with her terror, not her death. But in *The Sound and the
Fury* there are several allusions to Nancy's bones lying in
that ditch. We learn, however, that Roskus shot a crip-
pled mare named Nancy on that spot and that the children thought the vultures had stripped the horse's flesh
from the bones. The egg-and-omelette critics have ac-
cused Faulkner of creating "additional obfuscation" by
having two Nancies, one horse and one woman. This
again represents a failure to grasp the very nature of this
book. In life, animals and humans often have the same
names; and what Faulkner is recording is the process of
association: that ditch and the name Nancy (whether of
woman or horse) are forever linked in the memories of

the Compsons with death and decay and with that night of Nancy's strange terror. This is particularly significant in that the common memory of the Compson children in *The Sound and the Fury* centers around what occurred in the house at the time of their grandmother's death. The short story, although wholly separate from the novel, embodies within it the novel's central theme: in both tale and novel Faulkner is seeking to show childhood innocence, unaware of an adult world which it will come to know in its own measured time: the world of suffering and death, and bigotry and hatred and atrophy—and sound and fury.

Faulkner himself illuminated this theme in a charming statement during the literary seminar conducted by him in Japan in 1955. The transcript of the Nagano * meetings contains his reply to questions about his intention in *The Sound and the Fury* and the difficulty of the Benjy passages. This reply does not wholly help us with the novel's technical problems, which can be resolved only by attentive reading; but it has value as a post-factum account by an author of his creative thinking.

The Sound and the Fury, he tells us, began as a short story, a story without a plot, of some children being sent away from the house during the grandmother's funeral. They were too young to understand death, and they saw things only "incidentally to the childish games they were playing." Faulkner continues:

. . . and then the idea struck me to see how much more I could have got out of the idea of the blind, self-centeredness of innocence, typified by children, if one of those children had been truly innocent, that is, an idiot. So the idiot was born and then I became interested in the relationship of the idiot to the world that he was in but would never be able to cope with and just where could he get the tenderness, the help, to shield him in his innocence . . . And so the character of his sister began to emerge, then the brother, who, that Jason, (who to me represented complete evil. He's the most vicious character in my opinion I ever thought of). . . . Then it needs the protagonist, someone to tell the story, so Quentin appeared. By that time I found out I couldn't possibly tell that in a short story. And so I

* *Faulkner at Nagano* (Tokyo, 1956), pp. 102 *et seq.*

told the idiot's experience of that day, and that was incomprehensible, even I could not have told what was going on then, so I had to write another chapter. Then I decided to let Quentin tell his version of that same day, or that same occasion, so he told it. Then there had to be the counterpoint, which was the other brother, Jason. By that time it was completely confusing. I knew that it was not anywhere near finished and then I had to write another section from the outside with an outsider, which was the writer, to tell what had happened on that particular day [or occasion]. And that's how the book grew. That is, I wrote that same story four times. None of them were right, but I had anguished so much that I could not throw any of it away and start over, so I printed it in the four sections. That was not a deliberate *tour de force* at all, the book just grew that way. That I was still trying to tell one story which moved me very much and each time I failed, but I had put so much anguish into it that I couldn't throw it away, like the mother that had four bad children, that she would have been better off if they all had been eliminated, but she couldn't relinquish any of them. And that's the reason I have the most tenderness for that book, because it failed four times.

The book just grew that way. We could have no finer statement than this of Faulkner's intuition in his *anguishing* to convey the state of innocence of childhood. He ultimately achieved what he was looking for: long after the novel he wrote his short story of the children and their unawareness in "That Evening Sun Go Down." But the search for that story led him to the writing of a novel he rightfully cherished above his other works, even though he clothed it with the garments of "failure." It is failure if the reader reads it as the California teachers did, under the assumption that fictional narrative is fixed for all time and may never be scrambled or experimented with: that all fiction must be chronological and must have clarity for the lowest intelligence reading the book. We must turn our backs on such approaches to literature and recognize that as a novel of subjectivity, and as a novel of "point of view," *The Sound and the Fury* is perhaps the most remarkable of contemporary American novels. By its technical resources and symbolic strength Faulkner was enabled to perform in a work of art a great act of empathy—and of humanity.

CHAPTER IV

OBSERVATIONS

THE *nouveau roman* in France, strange as it may seem, stems from Dostoevsky and Kafka, Faulkner and the cinema, rather than from Joyce. The modern subjective movement in France has thus had a recent career quite distinct from that of the novel in England and America. Its first phase was that of Proust, which paralleled the vogue, if not the discoveries, of Joyce. Both Proust and Joyce were concerned with man's inner world; but there the resemblance ended. Proust was essentially reflective and analytic; Joyce was concrete and mimetic. Proust sought to recapture and retain that which had seemed to be evanescent. Joyce sought to represent the process of evanescence. Proust's quest was to discover and understand the beauty within man and his mode of perceiving it; the only beauty Joyce seems to have felt—it preoccupied him most of his life—was the beauty of words. By the same token, Proust rather than Joyce, was concerned with human relations in all their complexity and subtlety. Joyce has no real awareness of human relations; his people live within themselves.

This characterization of the two writers is not intended to diminish Joyce's historical influence; but it helps to suggest why the French were less responsive to him. They responded much more to Faulkner. He offered a fascinating and unfamiliar world, and used Joyce's inventions; these, within the labyrinth of *Ulysses*, had little meaning for the Gallic reader. The clutter of Dublin, conveyed through a verbal vaudeville, (that was, moreover, difficult to translate into French) had much less appeal than elemental passions, the nightmare of decay and guilt and obsessive lust, conveyed by the Southern writer. Faulkner's work was close to the deepest feelings of

France, especially after the decay of four years of German occupation. Conquered themselves, they could empathize with the sense of the long-ago conquered South, the lingering despair and demoralization which Faulkner's mental landscapes evoke. Moreover, Faulkner could breach the wall of a foreign language more easily than Joyce.

And then the French writers had charted states of feeling in fiction from the days of the epistolary novel, as in England. The French symbolists had taught a new generation how to use language evocatively, and how to listen to the music of the senses. Dujardin had performed the first modest experiment in full-scale subjectivity; and before him Flaubert had discovered how to create an illusion of simultaneity. Toward the Joycean *courant de la conscience* the French accordingly showed an understandable diffidence, a sophisticated detachment. We arrive thus at an historical paradox. The French, having originally influenced the modern movement in the English novel, did not respond in any serious way to what this influence created. Certainly not in the work of its chief artisan. In the fullness of time, skipping several stages, of our evolution, and absorbing other European influences, they have arrived at a point beyond Joyce. These seem to be the central historical facts.

The Edge of Consciousness

The French interest in Kafka stemmed from at least two sources. His innovations corresponded to the discontinuity and irrationality of their native nightmare, repeated thrice within a sixty-year span, and in the most recent time terminating in the arbitrary authority of a military occupation. And then the French had also fathered, doubtless through the same deep cause, movements such as surrealism, which reflected a search for the primary process of art, its primordial irrationality. The French rage for order, their need to explore, arrange, define (and the need further to find names for such explorations) in the end prevailed over the disorder. If there was the irrational in man, it could be discussed and cate-

178

gorized in a rational way; in the process, the gifted artists of this long-suffering country, could set down their notes from the underground. They could publish the lessons of absurdity in their midnight editions.

Franz Kafka has been regarded as an "objective" satirist. His novels have been taken as both literal and allegorical pictures of man's guilt and bewilderment before arbitrary authority. This is, however, only one side of his work; and it can be appreciated more completely if we become aware that its other side consists of a brilliant and apparently calculated externalization of whole areas of subjective experience. *The Trial* and *The Castle*, on analysis, show themselves as subjective novels: but the consciousness of the protagonist, in each case, has been turned inside-out. The seeming madness of the world of Kafka's Joseph K. (who feels guilty, but believes he isn't) and of the surveyor K., who cannot cope with the irrational authority of the Castle, resides in our being *inside* the consciousness of these characters. What Kafka has done has been to relate these inner stories as if they were occuring in a matter-of-fact outer world. He pays close attention to circumstantial detail—as if it were usual for a man to be arrested, yet not arrested; or for law courts to be located in attics; or for law books to contain pornographic pictures. The ever-present "assistants" of the surveyor in *The Castle*, who cannot be shaken off (put out of the door they climb back through the window, or show themselves there like the horses in "The Country Doctor"): they have separate identity, but they are in reality within, not outside, the surveyor. They are the "me" and the "not-me" of every man. We are within the character; and it is as if his entire interior world had been made as real to us as it seems to him; as if his nightmares were occuring in broad daylight in the very streets of town and city, visible to all.

This explains such strange episodes as the whippings at Joseph K.'s bank, or the curious sexual encounters which occur anywhere, indeed whenever the protagonist has a sexual fantasy. What makes Kafka difficult for the reader is that we do at times glimpse the outer world.

People do say rational things, and these are heard often through the distortions of the central character. It is not always easy to distinguish between the rational and the irrational in Kafka.

Kafka's nightmare atmosphere and his ambiguity of the actual and the imagined, is the real subject of the French *nouveau roman*. It is not possible to offer a detailed discussion of these complex new novels of the last decade; illustrative passages cannot be easily quoted as from Tolstoy or Joyce; we would be forced to quote fragments of fragments. For our purpose it suffices to suggest the essential qualities of this fiction. Like the stream-of-consciousness novels of the 1920's, plot ceases to be the author's concern; characters (in the old sense of described, acting individuals) disappear; people are suggested; we are given a gesture, a smile, an emanation from their minds, an emotion—but we seldom "see" them. We are in a novel of mirror atmospheres. Time in the Joycean novel was always the present. The new novel often simply uses the present tense, as if written in the language of a movie script. The objective world is described as in Kafka in a matter-of-fact way, often elaborately; but some of the novelists seek to avoid all emotion in the describing. The concrete is sought, sometimes with an obsessive monotony; it is this which gave rise to the term *objectivism*, where we would expect the novels to be called *subjectivism*. But for all their linear concretions, their effect is Kafkaesque; the concretions end up in the consciousness or within the sensual range of a human being. Instead of internal monologue we have undercurrents, fragments of thought, a marked discontinuity, a recurrent cinematic "cutting in" of verbal pictures.

These can be said to be some of the characteristics of the *nouveau roman* as written by Alain Robbe-Grillet, Claude Simon, and Michel Butor. Those of Nathalie Sarraute and Marguerite Duras in some respects come closer to the older forms of subjectivity; but even so, they are less sequential, and they remind us of Virginia

Woolf's "moments." Outer minutia is sometimes given in great detail, as in Butor; there is however also a kind of disfurnished world. Marguerite Duras can build a novel simply around two persons on a park bench. (She has dramatized Henry James's analogous tale of two personages, and their experience of a lifetime, "The Beast in the Jungle.")

The *nouveau roman* is often much narrower than the work of Joyce and Virginia Woolf, and less coherent. We look at fragmentary compositions, or a montage of faces, front and profile; or even at the geometry of Brancusi, as Mitchell Morse has suggested in his valuable essay on the "choreography" of the new French novel.* One inevitably turns to such terms as "choreography," or to the analogies of quasi-representational and fragmented art. Instead of creating the Joycean illusion of the clutter of consciousness, we are given "objective" fragments. The effect is still "non-objective."

Nathalie Sarraute in *L'ère du soupçon* and Robbe-Grillet in *Pour un nouveau roman*, with the talent which the French possess for theorizing about their practice of the arts, have been valuably articulate about the need for a "new novel." Proust (and even Joyce) are for them as old-fashioned as Dickens and Thackeray were to the Joyceans. Miss Sarraute, the most interesting and successful practitioner of a highly nuanced novel, does create, by the interest of her observation, a series of glimpses of different consciousnesses, caught in specific moments in time. Her work thereby conveys a sense of the human mystery and its solipsistic nature, but in an extremely narrow frame. We float from moment to moment. Conversation is "functional." We are always in a series of points of view. The pregnant phrase, the momentary remark, is revelatory of an inner world; at times we arrive at a series of what Joyce called his "epiphanies"—the moment of feeling caught on the wing, before it disappears into the backward reach of the lived life. Miss Sar-

* "The Choreography of the New Novel," *Hudson Review*, XVI, 3, (Autumn 1963)

raute, in a word, is no longer creating an illusion of reality; she seems to be attempting to render an illusion of appearances. She has written: "I study the psychological movements while they are forming, at the very moment of birth, so to speak, of reactions which cannot be perceived directly and clearly by the conscious mind, for the reason that they take place very rapidly somewhere on the extreme edge of consciousness." This is then the student of motivation but seeking its evidence in the peripheral vision, the eloquence of a glance, the significance of a pose. It has its roots, perhaps, in Freud's studies in the psychopathology of everyday life; although Miss Sarraute derives hers clearly from her own studies of the world around her. "It is these invisible but very real movements," she says (adding that they are numerous and complex), "which give meaning to our actions and to our words."

In attempting to put into language the unformed undercurrents of feeling that signal behavior, Miss Sarraute, has found herself in the same dilemma as her predecessors in the English-speaking world. Henry James, in his wish to remain within a limited point of view, soon enough began to fear that the reader might be lost in the process. He accordingly created what he called "the reader's friend," the *ficelle*-character, designed to act as a chorus, or to furnish a gloss, adding thus a dimension of vision to the story he could not otherwise convey. And James's explanation of the need for a "central intelligence" to illuminate action, to bring the maximum of perception to the given situation in such a novel, seems implied in Miss Sarraute's work. For she goes on to say that to succeed in reproducing these invisible reactions, it becomes necessary for her "to post another consciousness on the outer boundaries of the character's consciousness, one that is more clear-seeing than his own, and which records these movements as they develop, more or less in the manner of a movie-camera." She then adds: "I show them back then to the reader, in slow motion."

Readers doubtless will say that the motion in a Sarraute novel is indeed slow. But what is important is our discerning once again that in this journey to the outer boundaries of consciousness the omniscient author of the old novel still must name his surrogates, still must place the reader's eyes somewhere. The new novel, stemming from a different series of sources and events, encounters at bottom the same problems: those which Henry James long ago, and André Gide, more recently, dealt with in their experiments. Gide's *Counterfeiters*, in its self-conscious virtuosity, must be reckoned an important ancestor of the *nouveau roman*. His idea of having each chapter start as if he were beginning all over again, telling a new story; his use of the novel within the novel, the journal within the journal; his concern with multiple mirror-effects—these were a harbinger of the newest experiments.

Alain Robbe-Grillet is best known to the wider public by his *ciné-roman Last Year at Marienbad*, in which he used the camera as he does point of view—much to the bewilderment of the spectators. The cinema has in certain ways robbed the subjective novel of some of its novelty: it can achieve with great ease what the novelist must struggle to do within the straitjacket of language. Sound and sight can be conveyed to the spectator in actual—not approximate—simultaneity; the rapid succession of images, as well as the focusing upon minute and concrete detail, gives the cinema the power to "show" reality, not merely evoke it. Moreover, the camera-eye itself, constantly shifts the angles of vision. Out of such devices *Marienbad* was created. By these same means, Robbe-Grillet has built such novels as *La Jalousie* and *Le Voyeur*.

To say this however—to recognize the properties of the camera—is not to deny the power of words. One has only to photograph a given scene and then to juxtapose a text by a prose artist, to discover that the *affect* resides in the words rather than in the picture: the photograph, static or in motion, has indeed a vividness that invites no analogy with the vividness and power of words. It is a document: a moment frozen in time. The difference between word and picture might be illustrated in this fashion: there appeared in a newspaper once a photograph of a man walking in a snow-filled street in Harlem, taken as he passed under a large barbershop pole. It was a good clear shot. The caption in this instance, however, was taken from Ralph Ellison's *Invisible Man:*

The whole of Harlem seemed to fall apart in the swirl of snow. I imagined I was lost and for a moment there was an eery quiet. I imagined I heard the fall of snow upon snow. What did it mean? I walked, my eyes focused into the endless succession of barber shops, beauty parlors, confectionaries, luncheonettes, fish houses and hog-maw joints, walking close to the windows.

Here are two realisms. The realism of the photograph and the realism of language. The photograph is life, sharp, focused, real. And it feels just about as large as life, even though everything in it is reduced in size. The verbal realism is larger than life. The picture is fact. The words are feeling.

Robbe-Grillet would like very much to achieve naked "fact" in his prose. He addresses himself constantly to this end. He recognizes that the novel is a meeting of two experiences—the writer's and the reader's. He also insists that the work of fiction is itself an object, isolated, condensed, a package of words, a statement only of its own reality, enduring only so long as it is read. In a literal sense, this is true; save that the novel endures also within the *felt* sense of time within the reader: and this is what Robbe-Grillet seeks. One gets the impression that Robbe-Grillet would like to dissociate his own feelings and leave free rein to the reader's imagination. "Around us," he says, "defying the wolfpack of animist or thrifty adjectives, concrete things rear themselves. Their surface is smooth and clear and inviolate, and free from ambiguous reflection. All our literature has not succeeded in cutting one corner of it, or softening a single curve." But his wish to render an "impermeable world," we suspect will never be achieved. For no such world exists. Everything is in the eye of the beholder, even the camera eye, which takes its being from the eye of the photographer. Admirable perhaps in his desire to achieve super-objectivity, Robbe-Grillet ends in the subjective camp.* As Miss Sarraute remarks, "the language has not been found capable of expressing at one stroke what is seen in the wink of an eye; a whole being and myriads of minute moments can emerge in a few words, a single gesture, a chuckle . . ."

This comes closest to Virginia Woolf; and it is conceivable that students of these novels will at a later stage recognize that she, more than any other subjective novelist in English, long ago anticipated the new French experiments. To read the opening words of Simonne Jacquemard's *Night Watchman* is to feel oneself transported into Mrs. Woolf's world, if not her prose.

When dawn begins to separate leaves (*their lines will shoot forward to rediscover the traces of the day before, to occupy and intensify the sharp contours. . . .*) etc. etc.

a lengthy parenthesis of the kind Virginia Woolf used to bridge past and present. Mrs. Woolf tried to capture "the moment." Nathalie Sarraute speaks of "myriads of minute moments." Stendhal's mirror in the roadway has thus been broken into pieces; the reader is asked now to look into the minute fragments of the world reflected in them—reflected from the outer edge of consciousness.

A Multiplicity of Mirrors

"I have tried," says Lawrence Durrell of his *Alexandria Quartet*, "to turn the novel through both the subjective and objective modes." Three "movements" of his quartet are subjective. These are *Justine*, *Balthazar* and *Clea*. Between the last two Durrell has placed *Mountolive*, which is narrated conventionally. Darley, the teacher-writer—whose name rings but a slight change on the name of Durrell—narrates the subjective movements; but in *Mountolive* he becomes a character; he in turn is narrated, along with other characters, by an old-fashioned omniscient author. Durrellian subjectivity, we must add, is not stream-of-consciousness. It is set down in the auto-

* His preface to the script of *L'année derrière à Marienbad* offers an excellent analysis of the subjective-objective nature of cinema and the spectator's relation to what he sees on the screen.

biographical mode of Proust. Where Proust used only the memory of a single narrator, telling his story out of a personal past, Durrell offers a composite of memories of a whole group of characters. His novel imitates the method of biography as of autobiography.

All this presents no serious problem to a discussion of the formal aspects of his work. Durrell himself, however, has complicated discussion by using pseudoscientific terms. He speaks of his novel's "relativity" and of its being a "time-space soup-mix;" the recipe of his novel is, he says, "three sides of space and one of time." By this process he redivides his four movements in a manner different from the "subjective-objective." The first three parts, the subjective *Justine* and *Balthazar* and the objective *Mountolive*, are his space novels, "standing above time and turning slowly." Things here do not lead forward to other things; some lead backwards to things in the past. Only the subjective *Clea*, the last of the series, moves into the future. In a word, the "soup-mix" of "three and one" falls into one kind of arrangement for the space-time formula, and another for the subjective-objective formula.

We must distinguish carefully between the two formulas. If we think of the *Alexandria Quartet* in terms of space and time, the first three parts represent that questioning of the past which we call history. The final part, *Clea*, is told as actuality. In the first three, Darley-Durrell has removed himself to a Greek island to rethink and to tell of his Alexandria life in the period just before the second world war. "The picture I drew," he writes of *Justine*, "was a provisional one—like the picture of a lost civilization deduced from a few fragmented vases, an inscribed tablet, an amulet, some human bones, a gold smiling death-mask." The historian is aware of time's ruins. In *Clea*, however, the historian gives way to a kind of "deliverance from time" which is, in effect, a sequel to all that has been told before. The story-teller returns to Alexandria. His manner of telling remains subjective.

Of the four volumes which make up the *Quartet*, *Mountolive* and *Clea* have two separate functions. *Clea* breaks the stasis and takes place in time; *Mountolive* breaks the subjective mode and provides an objective point of reference. *Mountolive* is analogous to the Dilsey section in *The Sound and the Fury*. Faulkner, before Durrell, had used his subjective-objective "soup-mix," three parts subjective and one part objective. As Dilsey helps to complete the Compson family history "from the outside," *Mountolive* supplies important data hitherto absent from Darley's narrative (since it was unknown to him.)

Mountolive and the Dilsey section have the same function as Maria Gostrey in Henry James's *Ambassadors*. He called her "the reader's friend," and placed her in that novel as an aid to the central character, Lambert Strether. She helps him piece together his private inquiry into Chad Newsome's Parisian life, acting as a modern chorus in the story. *Mountolive* intervenes similarly as "chorus" for the entire *Quartet;* themes advanced in a hesitant way, are now stated without hesitation; needed backgrounds, social and political, become available to clear up the reader's confusion. This done, the story moves forward in time.

Durrell's subjective-objective method is intrinsic to the work; his time-space theorizing is extrinsic. The latter is, in reality, the critical-pedantic side of Durrell, like his novel-writing personage Pursewarden, mocking criticism and pedantry and offering intellectual concepts of the art of the novel. Small wonder that Clea, who is a painter, responds with anger in the final novel when Darley remarks he has been thinking of writing a volume of critical essays. "Criticism," she echoes—"as if the word were an insult"—and she smacks Darley "full across the mouth." The petty pedantries of the *Quartet*, the notes after the manner of Eliot in *The Waste Land*, the pretence of biographical scholarship, the lofty talk of relativity and time and space, are so much critical window-dressing in this series of novels, along with the epigraphs from de Sade and Freud. They amuse; they serve an atmospheric function for Darley, who seeks to "rebuild" Alexandria in his brain. We note that the academic apparatus is appended only to the subjective movements. *Mountolive*, being objective, requires no gloss and no context. When Durrell, in the preface to *Balthazar*, suggests that his time-space experiment is "not Proustian or Joycean method—for they [Proust and Joyce] illustrate Bergsonian 'duration' in my opinion and not 'space-time,' " he seems to be only throwing dust in the reader's eyes. The time-space concepts may not be Proustian or Joycean or Bergsonian; what we must recognize is that the all-important subjective-objective elements in his novel are.

If one is interested in attaching the *Alexandria Quartet* to certain contemporary fictional experiments, we would find looming large beside Proust and Joyce, André Gide's novel, *The Counterfeiters*, which employs the novelist-within-the-novel, notebooks and diaries, supplementary documents, unchronological narrative, various kinds of omniscience and a scrambling of the narrative, as in the Joycean school. Durrell's novel shows his complete absorption of contemporary fictional modes. He has nothing left to learn about "technique," and he has a superb command of the manipulation of point of view. Darley knows only that part of the story which happened to himself, and what he has gleaned from other sources. He writes his version of *Justine* and sends it to Balthazar; the latter adds his "interlinear," revealing many things of which Darley was not aware. Balthazar's point of view is thus superimposed upon, or placed beside, Darley's, who has also been drawing upon Arnauti's novel about Justine, and the posthumous papers of the novelist Pursewarden. Three novelists are busy in this novel, these two and Darley himself; not to speak of Durrell, who stage-manages the subjectivity and later intervenes as omniscient author.

This kind of virtuosity, as some critics have seen, has an hypnotic effect on the reader. There is surprise and mystification; things turn out, always, to have been somewhat different from what they seemed—and Durrell's genius for atmosphere is equal to the difficulties he has created for himself. (Indeed his poetry often runs away with him.) He draws on abundant "documentation": Clea's and Leila's letters, the three volumes of Justine's diary, Nessim's notes on his madness, the commentaries of Keats the newspaperman and of Capodistria, the poems of Cavafy, Pursewarden's jottings—all serve Darley-Durrell in the writing of "memorials" of the "unforgotten city," as they might a biographer. The subjective parts of the *Quartet* say to us again that man can only know a little of anything, that no two persons can have the identical vision. And that when someone thinks he really *knows*, there are a thousand and one little things which he will never know. Even when he is holding a woman in his arms, who seems to be one with him. Somewhere in the unconscious reaches of himself and of this woman there may be a love or loves that belong somewhere else.

This is the core of Durrell's "investigation of modern love" (as he puts it in his preface), for which he invokes all his skills, and which the Freudian epigraph proclaims —"I am accustoming myself to the idea of regarding every sexual act as a process in which four persons are involved. We shall have a lot to discuss about that." "Point of view" allows him to study the duplications and substitutions of love; the self-love (and self-contempt) Pursewarden shows when he sees his visage in a mirror and spits out his drink upon that image; later we will learn that he too has had an affair with Justine, which she masked by her affair with Darley; but which, in turn, masked Pursewarden's incestuous love for his blind sister, which (as with Quentin in Faulkner) leads him finally to take his life. The disguises of love are numerous, Durrell insists; and the disguises of memory no less numerous and no less deceptive. Durrell does not seek involuntary memory, like Proust; he uses the "iron chains of memory," "the supple tissues of human memory" and finds himself rewriting what he has remembered—and even readjusting remembered landscapes. Like Canaletto in Venice, he "rebuilds this city," and shifts the scenery a bit in other cities. Like all artists he improves on nature. If Trafalgar Square does not supply him with the trees he needs, he plants them there. His Alexandria, like Combray, is a work of the imagination.

Pursewarden dreams of an "N-dimensional novel" in which "the momentum forward is countersprung by references backward in time." Stephen Dedalus, moving through Dublin, suddenly remembers the sounds he once heard in Paris coming from the Bourse, a "gabble of geese," and thus makes a backward reference during his forward movement on Joyce's Bloomsday; and Peter Walsh, seeing Mrs. Dalloway after a long absence in India, performs that "marriage of the past and present" of which Durrell speaks—he remembers Clarissa as she was, and observes her as she is. Pursewarden's dream is thus not of a novel yet to be written, but of novels which have used time, association and memory precisely because this is the stuff of the inner vision. What Durrell achieves that is different from his predecessors is to make us aware of the presence of mirrors all around us, those actually on walls in rooms and barbershops, and those which we carry in our registering consciousness.

> I remember her [Justine] sitting before the multiple mirrors at the dressmaker's, being fitted for a sharkskin costume, and saying: "Look! five different pictures of the same subject. Now if I wrote I would try for a multi-dimensional effect in character, a sort of prism-sightedness. Why should not people show more than one profile at a time?"

And much later in the series Da Capo remarks:

> Today I had five girls. I know it will seem excessive to you. I was not trying to prove anything to myself. But if I said that I had merely blended five teas to suit my palate or five tobaccos to suit my pipe, you would not give the matter a second thought. You would, on the contrary, admire my eclecticism, would you not?

Da Capo's five girls, and Justine's five mirrors serve the same purpose: they are extensions of the self. One of the epigraphs from the Marquis de Sade used by Durrell implies the solipsism of his long novel: "The mirror sees the man as beautiful, the mirror loves the man; another mirror sees the man as frightful and hates him; and it is always the same being who produces the impressions."

It is Durrell's achievement that with all his bravura and his love for grand scenes and honeyed phrases, he has made us feel a time and a place and a group: and in the mid-century he has consolidated within his novels the subjective modes of the earlier decades. Where the *nouveau roman* has carried fragmentation still further, Durrell has kept his mirrors whole—and along the way devised many ingenious mirror-tricks.

Theatre of the Mind

Our concern has been with subjectivity in the novel; but it may be well to add a postscript on the influence of the subjective novel in the theatre. The dramatist is faced with materials less elastic than those of fiction; he has the same language as the novelist, but his words must accompany a visual image and they are written to be spoken. Today he knows that there is nothing he can do that cannot (in terms of technique and representation) be done more completely on the screen, though it is a question of how effectively. On the stage, the aside and the soliloquy had to serve for centuries, aided by the chorus, to place the audience close to the inner knowledge and life of a given character; and in recent time the use of flashback helped to enlarge a little the playwright's scope—without however altering the effect of solidity and concreteness that the stage, by its three dimensional nature, conveys. There is nothing more difficult to represent in the theatre than the dream state. Shakespeare's *A Midsummer's Night's Dream* suffers always from the mingling of poetry with stage carpentry; and the fairies, no matter how splendid the language that envelopes them, dance in their gauzy veils as fleshly beings. There have been dramatists who have sought the edge of consciousness and played with dreams. One need only mention Strindberg, or *Peer Gynt*, or the use of mood by Chekhov. But all this is still far removed from subjectivity as it has been practiced in our time in the novel.

Eugene O'Neill's experiment of the 1920's, *Strange Interlude*, in which his personages speak their inner thoughts in the midst of the traffic of the stage, resulted in a static dramatic confection. It captured the imagination of the audiences at the time, but it seemed dated and awkward during a recent revival. In reality O'Neill was using the soliloquies of the old plays; only the context of Freud and Joyce gave *Strange Interlude* an aura of the *avant-garde*. The subjectivity was entirely verbal; no use was made of the stage's visual properties. As in Joyce, language had to carry the entire burden, and O'Neill made no attempt (as he had done brilliantly in *The Emperor Jones*) to reproduce on the stage the mental images of the characters or to transpose into dramatic action the memories and thoughts contained in their soliloquies. *Strange Interlude* is thus rigid in its adherence to the novelist's method of rendering consciousness, and much less inventive and original than O'Neill had been in evoking the Emperor Jones's racial memories amid a crescendo of throbbing drums. In the earlier play he had intuitively used his scenic talent to suggest the primordial world of the self-elected Emperor; in the later play he flat-footedly imitated fiction.

Arthur Miller's *After the Fall*, given in New York in 1963 for the first time (that is thirty-five years after *Strange Interlude*), also derives from the stream of consciousness and internal monologue in fiction. Two works of fiction stand behind it: the unrelieved and vivid monologue of Albert Camus' *La Chute*, which may have contributed to Miller's title, and the inner monologue of Quentin Compson in *The Sound and the Fury*. The protagonist in *After the Fall* is named Quentin, and the program announces that "the action of the play takes place in the mind, thought and memory of Quentin, a contemporary man." Quentin takes his seat facing the audience; he has come to see someone, apparently a psychoanalyst, for he begins to talk of matters of intimate concern to himself—the kind of personal material that is usually brought to an analyst. Behind Quentin, on the stage, the scenes from his life and his memories, are acted out and given that visual concreteness which the stage cannot avoid, even when it tries to suggest evanescence. The best that can be offered is an illusion of the discontinuity of consciousness; and again and again Quentin steps out of his chair, and of his monologue, to re-enact his part in old scenes. These become flashbacks out of his past. As Miller puts it in his stage directions: "People appear and disappear instantaneously, as in the mind; but it is not necessary that they walk off stage. The dialogue will make clear who is 'alive' at any moment and who is in abeyance. The effect, therefore, will be the surging, flitting instantaneousness of a mind questing over its own surface and into its depths." In the production this was achieved with all the resources available in the modern theatre: personages (aided by the lighting) disappeared or faded from Quentin's "mind"—and the audience's vision—or emerged abruptly, without the traditional entrances and exits. And yet—so difficult is it to overcome the stage's rigidities—the effect was seldom that of time present; it was always memory, always in the past, even though occasionally Quentin's voice, assuming the form of the chorus, offered commentary from his seat in the present. The comments themselves were retrospective. The marriage between past and present was as uneasy as the marriages Quentin was describing to the audience.

The substance of *After the Fall* need not concern us here. The critics expressed their embarrassment at the closeness of Quentin's "confession" to the front-page facts of Arthur Miller's life; and Miller's own reply, that he had "imagined" the entire play, was ingenuous. For he was being reproached not for the failure to imagine, but to re-imagine (as all great artists have done) their personal experience. In substance, this autobiographical play approached at times the condition of *True Confession*, but in technique it could lay claim to being a serious attempt to represent inner life, within the essentially inflexible medium of the stage.

The play contained a certain number of vivid inventions: flashes from Quentin's childhood, recollections of fragments of talk, old phrases that lingered and reasserted themselves in the mind, scenes acted and re-enacted in the very way in which they obsessively force themselves upon memory. Miller was particularly successful in conveying to the audience Quentin's confusion of his mother with other women, and the intrusion of early juvenile experience into his adult behavior: this was done by simultaneous appearance of these women on different levels and at different depths upon the stage, within the use of the obsessive monologue of the narrator. All this testifies to the continuing vitality of this kind of experiment. What was unfortunate was that the material did not intrinsically possess vitality. There was no proper coalescence of form and substance; and by the time the dramatist reached the scenes between Maggie (the Marilyn Monroe figure in the play) and Quentin, the action relapsed into the old three-dimensional drama, the routine stage bickerings and quarrels between a husband and a wife to be found in a thousand plays. For long stretches we were in an ordinary drama, not in a stream of consciousness; Quentin and his monologue were removed to a secondary plane. The past re-enacted itself.

It was one of the imaginative qualities of James Joyce's night-town scenes in *Ulysses* that he knew how to make the reader feel that he was assisting at a drama of the mind, and participating in the fluidity of phantasmagoria. While it is difficult to quote this kind of material out of its context, let us for purposes of analogy, juxtapose a brief moment from Quentin's consciousness and one from that of Stephen Dedalus, as both recall their mother and a portion of their past.

Quentin, in his monologue, has just told of his meeting with Holga, the German girl he wants to marry. He remembers their having been at a café in Salzburg. And his memory brings into the foreground scenes with his first wife, Louise; this in turn brings up the image of his mother:

HOLGA: I feel sometimes . . . *Breaks off, then:* . . . that I'm boring you.

Louise appears.

LOUISE: I am not all this uninteresting, Quentin!

Louise is gone.

HOLGA: I really think perhaps we've been together too much.

QUENTIN: Except, it's only been a few weeks.

HOLGA: But I may not be all that interesting.

Quentin stares at her, trying to join this with his lost vision, and in that mood he turns out to the Listener.

QUENTIN: The question is power, but I've lost the connection.

Louise appears brushing her hair.

Yes!

He springs up and circles Louise.

I tell you, there were times when she looked into the mirror and I saw she didn't like her face, and I wanted to step between her and what she saw. I felt guilty even for her face! But ... that day ...

He returns to the café table and slowly sits.

... there was some new permission ... not to take a certain blame. There was suddenly no blame at all but that ... we're each entitled to ... our own unhappiness.

HOLGA: I wish you'd believe me, Quentin; you have no duty here.

QUENTIN: Holga, I would go. But the truth is, I'd be looking for you tomorrow. I wouldn't know where the hell I thought I had to be. But there's truth in what you feel. I see it very clearly; the time does come when I feel I must go. Not toward anything, or away from you. But there is some freedom in the going. ...

Mother appears, and is raising her arm.

MOTHER: Darling, there is never a depression for great people! The first time I felt you move, I was standing on the beach at Rockaway. ...

Quentin has gotten up from the chair, and, moving toward her:

QUENTIN: But power. Where is the ..?

MOTHER: And I saw a star, and it got bright, and brighter, and brighter! And suddenly it fell, like some great man had died, and you were being pulled out of me to take his place, and be a light, a light in the world!

QUENTIN: *to Listener:* Why is there some . . . air of treachery in that?

FATHER: *suddenly appearing—to Mother:* What the hell are you talking about? We're just getting a business started again, I need him!

> *Quentin avidly turns from one to the other as they argue.* *

Stephen Dedalus, in the brothel in Dublin's night-town, and in his blurred and drunken visions, has remembered his father saying "Think of your mother's people." The allusion to the mother recalls his talk earlier in the day with Buck Mulligan, and Mulligan's reproaches at his refusal to pray beside his mother's death-bed. In this passage Stephen's guilt, like Quentin's, gives a particular cast to the visions:

(Stephen whirls giddily, Room whirls back. Eyes closed, he totters. Red rails fly spacewards. Stars all around suns turn roundabout. Bright midges dance on wall. He stops dead.)

STEPHEN
Ho!

(Stephen's mother, emaciated, rises stark through the floor in leper grey with a wreath of faded orange blossoms and a torn bridal veil, her face worn and noseless, green with grave mould. Her hair is scant and lank. She fixes her bluecircled hollow eyesockets on Stephen and opens her toothless mouth uttering a silent word. A choir of virgins and confessors sing voicelessly.)

THE CHOIR
> *Liliata rutilantium te confessorum . . .*
> *Iubilantium te virginum . . .*

(From the top of a tower Buck Mulligan, in particoloured jester's dress of puce and yellow and clown's cap with curling bell, stands gaping at her, a smoking buttered split scone in his hand.)

BUCK MULLIGAN
She's beastly dead. The pity of it! Mulligan meets the afflicted mother. *(He upturns his eyes.)* Mercurial Malachi.

THE MOTHER
(With the subtle smile of death's madness.) I was once the beautiful May Goulding. I am dead.

* Arthur Miller, *After the Fall* (New York, 1964), Act Two, 72–73.

STEPHEN

(*Horrorstruck*) Lemur, who are you? What bogeyman's trick is this?

BUCK MULLIGAN

(*Shakes his curling capbell.*) The mockery of it! Kinch killed her dogsbody bitchbody. She kicked the bucket. (*Tears of molten butter fall from his eyes into the scone.*) Our great sweet mother. *Epi oinopa ponton.*

THE MOTHER

(*Comes nearer, breathing upon him softly her breath of wetted ashes.*) All must go through it, Stephen. More women than men in the world. You too. Time will come.

STEPHEN

(*Choking with fright, remorse and horror.*) They said I killed you, mother. He offended your memory. Cancer did it, not I, Destiny.

THE MOTHER

(*A green rill of bile trickling from a side of her mouth.*) You sang that song to me. *Love's bitter mystery.* *

We must make allowance for the essential difference between these passages: Miller's addressed to production on the stage, Joyce's intended, in spite of the dramatic form, for the reader's eye, and using stage directions as a form of narrative. The theatre, save in the old poetic plays, is wedded to hard prose; and in neither O'Neill nor Miller do we find the poetry required to lift their pictures of consciousness away from the weight of the scenery. To say this is to suggest their particular limitations, and to recognize, what we have seen throughout this study, that it requires a fund of poetic power to express the dialectic of the mind. The time will perhaps come when there will be a poet in the theatre capable of inventing, for the theatre-form, certain of the devices Joyce found for the novel-form. It will require the finest kind of dramatic poet. Modern stagecraft alone cannot accomplish it. Until such a man appears, the stage will have to recognize that the novel's modes of subjectivity are proper to the novel. They do not easily serve other forms.

* James Joyce, *Ulysses* (New York, 1934), 564–565.

197

A LOGIC OF SUBJECTIVITY

When I wrote the first part of this book a decade ago, it seemed as if the subjective novel had reached its term. Art understands art: and writers as different as Virginia Woolf and William Faulkner, H. D., and Conrad Aiken had cut through the thick padding of Joyce's exuberant pedantry and recognized at once the new dimensions he had opened up for the novel. The first part of this book defined these dimensions and explained them in the light of literary history. The ensuing pages offered certain further observations on modes of subjectivity and the evolution of this kind of fiction since Joyce.

It might be useful to ask ourselves again what the subjective novel accomplishes that cannot be accomplished by old-fashioned narrative method, and more important still, why such fiction must be read in a new way. The author's purpose in the subjective novel is to place the reader within the consciousness of a character. This never occurs in quite the same way in the traditional novel. In the latter the author is present; he tells the story usually about certain people and the events of their lives. In the subjective novel the author—as Joyce put it—is "refined out of existence" and the people are made to tell their own story, in their own way, not in the author's way. They tell it for one thing in a discontinuous way. Hence from the moment a novelist places his reader in someone else's consciousness, strange things begin to happen in fiction: a chain of action, a particular and logical process, is started which did not exist in the old novels; and if we understand this process, we begin to realize what is meant when I speak of "new dimensions" in story-telling.

For convenience's sake, I have divided this new rationale or logic—the logic of subjectivity—into four steps.

They are simple enough when we name them; they become very complex when we try to describe them. When we are in a stream-of-consciousness we begin by being committed inescapably to the *point of view* of the particular consciousness; we become involved with its *discontinuity* or scrambled state; we discover that things can occur *simultaneously* in it (as they do in our daily experience); and finally we find ourselves in a *continuous* present outside of history. Point of view, discontinuity, simultaneity, time—these are useful headings for our study of modes of subjectivity in modern fiction.

Point of view: The reader finds himself placed behind the eyes of the character, thinking the character's thoughts and looking out upon the world through the character's eyes. He has also acquired all the senses of the character. He not only sees, but touches, smells, hears in the particular way of this character; he is endowed, in a word, with his feelings. This occurs in the most direct fashion imaginable: that is through an illusion created out of language that we have become the particular consciousness—and no other—even while our own consciousness is either held in the background or is mingling with it. We are within a continuous counterpoint of rational thought and fleeting peripheral impressions, the focused and unfocused record of the senses. Within such a range of perceptual experience, many kinds of novelistic and poetic illusions may be attempted.

Discontinuity: This follows from the moment the author has transferred the reader into his character's consciousness. There are many ways of handling "point of view." It can be conveyed wholly in terms of the reasoning, exploring, pondering mind; it can seek the peripheral areas of that mind; it can mix the two; it can even attempt the more difficult rendering of unverbalized feeling, that is it can take the form, as Northrop Frye puts it, "of speeches of characters constructed precisely out of what they do *not* say, but what their behavior and attitudes say in spite of them." This is what Virginia Woolf tried to do in such a novel as *The Waves* or what we encounter in Faulkner's *As I Lay Dying;* and it is what the *nouveau ro-*

man is attempting in France. The subjective novel can render memory and association in the methodical and searching manner of Proust, or in the disordered discontinuous manner of Joyce, or as Conrad Aiken handles it in certain brilliant oratorical monologues in *Great Circle*. The Joycean method arranges for us an impression of unsorted thought and perception amid the clutter of a given day. Joyce paid close attention however to the "trigger" mechanisms, the smells or sounds or random perceptions which give rise to a given thought or memory. In other words the symbolist theory of "correspondences" enters into play in such creation, even while the novel obeys also the psychology of stimulus and response.

When discontinuous experience is recorded, the reader assumes a burden of reading that does not exist in traditional fiction, where he may confide himself wholly to the all-knowing story-teller. In the subjective novel the author ceases to be all-knowing. He knows (or pretends to know) no more than his character; and if that character be an idiot like Benjy, he is reduced to the sign language and the anarchy of the senses. He also, on occasion, must supply the words for that which is wordless.

Simultaneity: Possessing only words, which must be set down in a continuum, the author must arrange this continuum to make the reader feel that he is hearing certain sounds at the very moment that he is thinking thoughts. As in Tolstoy's handling of the various "simultaneous" levels of the horse race in *Anna Karenin*, or the moments in *Ulysses* when Joyce makes us aware of the many simultaneous pulses of Dublin, the reader is made to feel life not as something two dimensional and unilinear, but as a series of multiple moments within the moment.

Time: We are no longer in time past, in that "once upon a time" which most story-tellers use. It is nearly always here and now in subjective fiction. The reader reads the thoughts and the senses at whatever moment they are thought or sensed. This gives the stream of consciousness novel a sense of immediacy. Time in these novels is psychological, since they are concerned (as Auerbach puts it) with "a sharp contrast between the brief span of time occupied by the exterior event and the dreamlike wealth of a process of consciousness which traverses a whole subjective universe." Mechanical time is present, as it is in our daily lives, with every ticking watch and every chiming clock. But there is also inner time which takes no stock of clock time.

This is the particular logic in the representation of subjectivity. Our four steps are not necessarily successive; there are many ways of combining and recombining them. Each novelist who writes in the subjective mode can be studied for his particular way of showing inner vision. Different writers have had to seek different modes to express the elusive flame-like quality of thought.

2

What are the limitations of subjective fiction? Certain things are gained—certain things are lost. It is a world of fragments, of glimpses, atmospheres. Character, as we know it in the old novels, is dissolved into environment. Mrs. Ramsay, in *To the Lighthouse*, is visible as a series of feelings, a creature observed through her own emotions and those of other personages, who are themselves described only through limited areas of perception. Durrell's *Justine* looks out at us from five mirrors at the same time. We are transposed into a relative rather than a fixed vision.

Few novelists, it must be recognized, possess the language necessary for such writing. And very few the power. Henry James saw this long ago, when he was a mere twenty-one, writing his first reviews. "To project yourself into the consciousness of a person essentially your opposite requires the audacity of great genius and even men of genius are cautious in approaching this problem." Browning, James observed, never assumed the voice of his characters for more than a few pages at a time.

At times the difficulties created for us in reading stream-of-consciousness are akin to those a modern generation has encountered in the plastic arts. The reader is "trapped" in the given point of view; he gains a limited experience. He is perhaps as helpless as the spectator facing a non-representational canvas. Many of the limitations may seem to be there if we look at them in terms of the fiction to which we are accustomed. We cannot really invoke Tolstoy in order to dismiss Joyce, any more than we can summon Rembrandt in order to do away with Picasso. We are still left with the critic's job of work: of taking a good look both at Joyce and Picasso. True criticism, as we know, has never used a single yardstick.

3

C. P. Snow's recurrent attacks on the subjective novel have enlivened the discussion of this form of fiction in recent years. His principal American lecture on this subject appeared in the *Kenyon Review* in 1961; it is a highly polemical article and the details of his argument need not concern us. His main purpose was to suggest that there has been too much attention paid to Joyce and not enough to Tolstoy and Proust. The passage which does concern us, however, is his expression of surprise that the subjective movement and its innovations "caught hold of literary sensibility." It may, indeed, be difficult for a man trained in science to accept a type of fiction which contains discontinuity and which scrambles its data; which in other words seems to be all clutter and chaos; but this is the way of consciousness, and one would have been even more surprised if the literary sensibility of our time had ignored the attempt of fiction to use symbolist methods and approach the condition of poetry.

By the same token, Snow's attempt to explain the vogue of stream-of-consciousness as a conspiracy of the "new critics," who found it apt subject for exegesis, hardly meets the historical conditions that produced *Ulysses.* Erich Auerbach admirably describes these conditions in *Mimesis:* "At the time of the first world war and after, in a Europe unsure of itself, overflowing with unsettled ideologies and ways of life, and pregnant with disaster—certain writers distinguished by instinct and insight find a method which dissolves reality into multi-

202

ple and multivalent reflections of consciousness. That this method should have been developed at this time is not hard to understand."

We can, by extension, apply this line of thought to what has happened in fiction since the second world war. Faced now not with disintegration, but with a serious threat of dissolution, the novelist has turned away from the fragmenting of experience described by Auerbach. He has rediscovered the picaresque and the comic and sought old forms that will give him as much of a grasp as possible on the concrete and the palpable. Or he has written philosophical novels; or created anti-novels out of his sense of emptiness and despair. The novel, as we can see, has been sensitive to the essential historical conditions—the very mood and atmosphere—of our time.

However, as we have seen, even within this more recent turning away from inner reality, certain writers have continued to experiment with modes of subjectivity. Whenever the novel tries to follow the path of reportage and of journalism, the correcting force of the imagination and of poetry intervene to preserve it from becoming as commonplace as the daily newspaper. Naturalism has proved to be limited in the extreme; Zola remains, but his followers are dull fellows, and his imitators on the American scene during the 1930's are all but forgotten. The novelists of large poetic imagination have always prevailed. And the most original novelists of our time remain those of the first half of the century. James and Proust and Joyce—on the largest plane—and a grade below them Kafka and Mrs. Woolf and Faulkner. One could add a long list of the non-experimental writers, like Mann, or Forster, or D. H. Lawrence, who loom large, but discussion of them belongs elsewhere. In the backward reach of this century, the fictional explorers remain those who have reached more deeply into consciousness. This is wholly understandable, for this has been the century of psychology; and the novel, as we know, has always been first and foremost "psychological."

INDEX

INDEX

208

209

Verlaine, Paul, 95
Vico, Giovanni Battista, 29, 80

Wagner, Richard, 92, 115
Wells, H. G., 16, 49, 74, 154-55, 157
West, Rebecca, 39, 90
Wharton, Edith, 22
Wilson, Edmund, viii, 31, 38
Woolf, Virginia, v, vii, 29, 94, 103-4, 124-36, 137, 140, 142, 153-55, 170, 171, 180-81, 185, 198, 203; *Jacob's Room,* 135; *The Mark on the Wall,* 134-35; *Mrs Dalloway,* 25, 101, 124, 128, 131-35, 147; *Night and Day,* 127; *To the Lighthouse,* 97, 128, 130, 201; *The Voyage Out,* 103, 127; *The Waves,* 199
Wordsworth, William, 126, 155

Zola, Émile, 31, 133, 203

OTHER TITLES IN THE

Universal Library

EDITED BY LEON EDEL

FRENCH POETS AND NOVELISTS, by *Henry James*

The first American edition of a classic work of criticism, including
extended essays on such major figures as Flaubert, Balzac, Baudelaire, George Sand, Turgenev, Alfred de Musset, Théophile Gautier,
and Sainte-Beuve. As Professor Edel remarks in his introduction:
"No critic in the nineteenth century stood on firmer ground in his
analysis of fiction.... The papers on Balzac and Turgenev, George
Sand and Flaubert remain among the finest in the English language
devoted to French writers."

UL 164 $1.95

Also available in hardcover edition $4.00

GHOSTLY TALES OF HENRY JAMES

A volume of James' "apparitional" tales, selected and edited by
Professor Edel, including:

> The Romance of Certain Old Clothes
> The Ghostly Rental
> Sir Edmund Orme
> De Grey: A Romance
> The Friends of the Friends
> The Turn of the Screw
> Owen Wingrave
> The Real Right Thing
> The Third Person
> The Jolly Corner

UL 161 $2.25

A SELECTED LIST OF TITLES IN THE
Universal Library

HISTORY AND POLITICAL SCIENCE

LITERATURE, CRITICISM, DRAMA, AND POETRY

PSYCHOLOGY

TITLES OF GENERAL INTEREST